YOU
DO
KNOW

'An astonishing book that takes you through how intuitive thinking can improve your life and change the world. If you think you know everything there is to know about intuition, know again!'

David R. Hamilton PhD

'Becky's no-nonsense approach to intuition enables readers to easily comprehend every point she makes. And what makes this read unique is the very personal experience upon which it is based.'

Chris Hawkins, BBC Radio

'Becky Walsh's marvellous book taught me to trust my intuition, something I've always ignored in the past, most often to my own detriment. In a very accessible and at times comical way, Walsh shows you how to listen to your inner knowing to ensure that every decision you make in life is the right one. Trust your intuition – read this book!'

Debbie Chazen, actress and comedian

First published and distributed in the United Kingdom by:
Hay House UK Ltd, 292B Kensal Rd, London W10 5BE.
Tel.: (44) 20 8962 1230; Fax: (44) 20 8962 1239.
www.hayhouse.co.uk

Published and distributed in the United States of America by:
Hay House, Inc., PO Box 5100, Carlsbad, CA 92018-5100.
Tel.: (1) 760 431 7695 or (800) 654 5126;
Fax: (1) 760 431 6948 or (800) 650 5115.
www.hayhouse.com

Published and distributed in Australia by:
Hay House Australia Ltd, 18/36 Ralph St, Alexandria NSW 2015.
Tel.: (61) 2 9669 4299; Fax: (61) 2 9669 4144.
www.hayhouse.com.au

Published and distributed in the Republic of South Africa by:
Hay House SA (Pty), Ltd, PO Box 990, Witkoppen 2068.
Tel./Fax: (27) 11 467 8904.
www.hayhouse.co.za

Published and distributed in India by:
Hay House Publishers India, Muskaan Complex, Plot No.3, B-2,
Vasant Kunj, New Delhi – 110 070.
Tel.: (91) 11 4176 1620; Fax: (91) 11 4176 1630.
www.hayhouse.co.in

Distributed in Canada by:
Raincoast, 9050 Shaughnessy St, Vancouver, BC V6P 6E5.
Tel.: (1) 604 323 7100; Fax: (1) 604 323 2600

Text © Becky Walsh, 2013

The moral rights of the author have been asserted.

A catalogue record for this book is available from the British Library.

ISBN 978-1-78180-100-0

Printed and bound by TJ International Ltd, Padstow, Cornwall

YOU
DO
KNOW

LEARNING TO ACT ON
INTUITION
INSTANTLY

BECKY WALSH

HAY HOUSE

HAY HOUSE

Australia • Canada • Hong Kong • India
South Africa • United Kingdom • United States

CONTENTS

ACKNOWLEDGMENTS

Mostly, creating a book feels like sitting on your own in a room with your thoughts. However, it is who and what influences those thoughts, who gives you the love and space to put them to paper, and who gives you the breaks to get them published. All of these people and their energy are with you in the birth of a book.

So with gratitude to all of those lifelong accumulating insights given in random ways, but in more direct ways I would like to thank:

Cat Knott for her unwavering support and friendship. My family, Cohort Y; the tutors and faculty at the California Institute of Internal Studies; Will Swift, Alexia Marcou, Heena Prajapat, Mark Sherwood, Syd Martin, Anna Bullard, Linda Chard, Liz Dean, Jo Sharp, Samantha Kelly, Briana Le Bold, Marlo McKenzie, Kate Orr, and John Purkiss. Everyone at Hay House, including Michelle Pilley, Sandy Draper, and Jo Burgess.

Introduction
IT'S NOT MAGIC AND YET...

A few years ago I was sitting in the departure lounge at London's Heathrow airport waiting for my flight to San Francisco to be called. In the couple of months before, I had sold my home and with it the new kitchen (I had saved eight years for!), given away my belongings, ended a relationship and, despite being at the height of my career, I was leaving that, too, and going back to college. I couldn't at the time tell you why, I *knew* why, but I had no logical or rational reason for my actions. All I can tell you is I was following my intuition and it has ultimately led to this book being in your hands.

So if I had a magic wand, I would give you one life transformative gift, a gift that would allow you to have faith in yourself, build deep openhearted relationships, make brave and inspired decisions, and know who to trust. In fact, if I had a magic wand, I might just use it to poke you in the ribs because you already have that gift; it is your intuition.

For many years I have worked as an intuitive catalyst. Most of my clients come to see me because they are coming up against blocks or holding points that are stopping them: being who they want to be; living the life they want; or understanding their most important relationships. Using intuition, psychology, spiritual disciplines, and a bit of life coaching I give them the tools and information for change. The truth is that I'm often told I am reaffirming something they *already* knew. All I am doing is putting into words something they knew inside, but had no words for. So in writing this book I am about to do myself out of a job, because in this book I am going to show you that YOU *DO* KNOW!

It pains me that there are so many people going through life feeling lonely, disconnected, unheard, not trusting themselves, or lacking self-belief. Knowing what I know about intuition, I can see that this doesn't have to be the case. When I look back over my life the things I remember most are not the places I've been but the time I spent in the joy of other people's company. It is part of the human condition to want to feel a loving connection to other people. After all, it is what all the great love songs are about.

Many people struggle to keep their hearts open to love. There is a very good reason for this, too, as the chances are that in your lifetime you have been hurt, shut down, shut up, and shut off. I can say this wholeheartedly as I see it in my clients every day. Yet if I asked you when you first suspected a situation or person would hurt you, the likelihood is that you already knew from the very beginning: when you first met the perpetrator or found yourself in the situation that subsequently went wrong. Yet you still allowed your mind and therefore your ego to govern your decision-making. The revolution comes when your intuition becomes stronger than the fear generated by your ego. When you don't work from the ego, other people can't control you and you can't be paralyzed by fear.

Forgive me for making a generalization and presuming that you're not already living life intuitively. To be clear, I am not talking about the kind of intuition that has been taught or experienced so far. This is a new understanding of intuitive knowing, one that doesn't involve your ego – that's the voice in your head that thinks it 'knows' what's best… I am talking about a knowing without words that comes from deep inside you when you've managed to make your ego stop talking for just a minute and tune in to the softer, authentic tune of your intuition.

My challenge is writing a book about a 'knowing' without words and having to use words to do so. This book brings together many empowering ideas, some of which you might already be aware, which can be carried from one generation to the next. This form of evolutionary intuition is revolutionary: it draws on psychology, spirituality, and self-development. You may find as you read the following pages that you feel a sense of 'I *knew* that,' with a knowing deep inside of you but, perhaps, have never had the words to express it before.

Not to put too fine a point on it, **to live intuitively is to live in freedom**. When you know how to trust your intuition, you have much more control over your ego, over your fear, and can learn to live in happy abundance.

We live in a magical world of possibility. When they understand it correctly and see beyond the humdrum of 'everyday' living, most people get excited about the idea of developing their intuition. However, this is not a paranormal or extraordinary ability, it's a life skill. This was clearly illustrated by Thomas J. Stanley (PhD) who studied the behaviors, habits, and mindsets of 733 millionaires and multimillionaires for his book *The Millionaire Mind,* and discovered that the number-one reason that people became successful in business was 'Ideas through intuition.'

Years of research have led me to the same profound understanding of the power of intuition in relationships, family, decision-making and ethical business. I don't just know it; I live it.

This book is full of survival skills for the changing world. This is not a passive evolution; it is an active revolution for peace.

Chapter 1
HOW WE RECEIVE INTUITION

There is one dilemma that plagues most people who want to live an intuitive life, '*how* do I know when it is my intuition?' It's an important question as there are many factors at play in the human psyche when we make a decision. We can get intuition confused with:

- Blind desperate hope: mostly when it comes to relationships we look for intuitive signs to tell us that the person we have a crush on is in fact 'the one.' If the man of our dreams is called Mack, then every MACK truck that passes us on the road becomes A SIGN! A bit like pulling petals off a daisy saying 'she loves me, she loves me not' and deciding as it lands on 'not' that the daisy is clearly broken.

- Fear: being scared of not being able to do the job can cause 'I have a bad feeling about taking this job' or not being bothered enough to take the learning curve it requires.

- Misguided optimism: I want this job so badly I *know* it's mine!

- Past experience: having a bad feeling about someone because he or she reminds you of someone who hurt you before means that we can project our past experience on to them.

- Making it fit: 'The psychic told me I would come into some money, and then my mother died and left me her house.'

- And imagination: the ability to be able to make sense of the world through a mind process of creative storytelling, visualization, ideas formed into pictures, and daydreams. Everything you see around you started in someone's imagination. We can't create without it, yet some of these skills have a part to play in intuition, as your intuitive knowing uses your imagination to 'create' the knowing into pictures – this is known as clairvoyance. However, sometimes it can seem tricky to distinguish between imaginative fantasy and intuitive knowing.

In fact, there are only two forms of intuitive knowing: one you can trust and the other requires a deeper inquiry into its origin – and is the voice of the ego. That's important knowledge because all of the factors listed above (apart from imagination) come from the ego part of the mind and are not intuition. In the next chapter you will learn about both and how to tell the difference between the two. Unlike other forms of information, intuitive knowing isn't something you get through effort; you relinquish your barriers and allow the insight to come to you.

The four types of intuition

Let's start by taking a look at how we receive intuitive insight. Note I say receive as it's not possible to 'go out and get' intuitive information. Think of it this way: if you stuck an intuition satellite dish to your third eye, you would still have to be tuned into the right station to get a picture. The problem is we are sending out information all the time so we miss what intuition is giving us. It is the same as talking and listening at the same time; it's very hard to do, unless you are someone's mother. Mothers and grandmothers seem to be able to do that; at least mine can.

There are four main ways that people who are open can receive intuitive information. To be in balance it is important to have a little of each of the types, or at least to practice the other skills until you do.

1. Mental intuition

A mental intuitive will receive 'downloads' of intuitive information into the creative part of their mind and can almost express it without finding the words first. A simple explanation is that the part of the brain most commonly understood to be creative is the right hemisphere (more on that in the next chapter). An upside of being a 'mental intuitive' is that you are often sure when you make a decision. A downside is that people will accuse you of thinking too much and, although mental intuitives are great communicators, if they don't mix their intuition with empathy can sometimes be a bull in a china shop with information.

Student case study: The clairvoyant

One of the exercises that my students love is to create postcard paintings with wax and an iron. All the colors splurge together and the wax melts onto the postcard making new colors, textures, and shapes. The students then swap pictures and read them as if the person had just painted a picture of their life onto the card. The exercise allows the right hemisphere of the brain to get to work, which activates the intuitive mind. Most students report feeling that they are just 'making it up.' Only when the receiver of the information remarks on the accuracy do they start to believe their insights.

Helen, although not the most confident of students, starts slow then gets into a flow of communication that seems to bypass her logical mind. Her speech speeds up, her facial animation increases, and she loses herself in the flow of consciousness coming from her lips. As the information slows down, she looks back at the card that inspired her to access the download. She then turns a little self-conscious and asks a fellow student stunned at her accuracy: 'Was any of that right?'. Helen sees pictures in her mind (clairvoyance) and has downloads of information. In her everyday life she is brilliant at analyzing, putting patterns together, and thinking outside the box.

2. Somatic intuition

A somatic intuitive feels intuition physically, meaning that their body is a receiver of information. Somatic intuitives feel deeply that they are part of nature. They learn to know what all the subtle sensations mean in their body and can act upon them. An upside of being a somatic intuitive is that you remain grounded. You're able to react quickly and without panicking in physically threatening situations. A downside is that your body is always 'talking' to you and will use all aspects of physicality to explain any emotional discord in you and others. A somatic intuitive might be the person who finds it impossible to hold out to the third date: they want to get to know someone with their body before they get to know their personality.

Student case study: The mover

When I was a student at the California Institute of Integral Studies we learned that there are many ways to complicate things by using words. The course involved one weekend at college every few weeks; the rest of the degree was home study. At the start of each weekend, we took turns to talk about how we were doing with the course and our lives. One overseas student often found trying to communicate in a second language frustrating. Her English was excellent, but she lacked the speed of speaking in her native tongue. Then, one day, while trying to explain, she just got up and danced. The whole room became electric. There was no need for words; we knew and could feel exactly how she felt.

You might have had this experience while watching an actor on stage, a dance piece, live music, or even in the movie theater. You might have experienced it as your hairs standing on end, a feeling in your belly, something 'put your back up, without reason,' or as a sensation that comes from nowhere. It could be when you're driving and your foot comes off the gas without thinking, giving you valuable seconds to react to something up ahead. Being connected to the physical signals of your body is vitally important. It is your body that makes all of your hopes and dreams even possible, and it is communicating with you all the time. When you are busy thinking about how to solve a problem, you might find the answer comes more quickly if you let go and dance.

3. Emotional intuition

An emotional intuitive, also known as an 'empath,' feels things empathically. They pick up other people's emotions and sometimes find it hard not to make choices for others rather than for themselves. An upside of being an emotional intuitive is that you are very attractive to people. You understand people on a deeper level than most. The downside is that you find it hard to communicate who you are to people. If love were in measures, your love fills a highball glass and the love of others fills a shot. Everyone loves to his or her capacity, but you can still feel disappointed as your cup overflows and theirs goes down in one gulp.

Student case study: The empath

In a circle setting I like to ask my students to put an object into a box. The object has to be something they wear or use every day such as a watch, a piece of jewelry, keys, or even a phone. Then I get each student to take out one of the objects, hold it in their hand and, without knowing who the object belongs to, say a few things about that person. We then reveal the owner and return the item. This is known as 'psychometry' (and it is a fantastic way of finding out your intuitive type). The object absorbs the energy of the owner and can be intuitively read by someone holding it. I always stress, however, that whatever you feel from the object you must end what you're saying on a positive note.

One of my students, Carl, is extremely empathic. He took hold of a lady's watch and proceeded to talk about how the owner was feeling emotionally. He talked about the inner sadness that had followed her since childhood, and how he sensed her reaching out but still feeling very alone. The room started to become heavy and take on the feelings from his words. Carl ended by saying 'I would go as far as saying the owner of this watch is depressed.' As the teacher about to reveal the owner of this watch I was cringing. There were two possibilities; she would say 'yes that's all true,' burst into tears, and leave the room never to be seen again; or deny everything and Carl would think he wasn't very good at psychometry. So I asked Carl to leave his insights on a positive note. He paused and said 'It's a nice watch.'

Empaths really do feel other people's emotions very deeply. Most students of intuition are looking for what they can do to help others; therefore we look for others' pain rather than the joy in their hearts. What Carl learned later was how to use his intuition to look out for evidence of how the watch-owner had survived and thrived at many other points in her life, and to remind her of who she really was, so that he could end his observation with empowerment.

4. Spiritual intuition

Connected to a collective consciousness, a spiritual intuitive has a sensitive awareness of the energy system around his or her body – their 'aura.' They can't always put this knowing into words, but if you're in the desert and in need of water then this is the person to follow. We are all in an energy bubble of constant communication and a spiritual intuitive can access this information. The upside of being a spiritual intuitive is that you have a wonderfully creative imagination. The downside is that you are often ungrounded and seen by others as being flaky.

Student case study: The spiritual intuitive

Have you ever been accused of having your head in the clouds? If so, you might just be a spiritual intuitive. With my students I often talk through ideas then set a task so they can experience for themselves what I've said. A spiritual intuitive will always ask me

'What are we doing?' It is not just that they weren't listening; they weren't even in the room! Often accused of being ungrounded, a spiritual intuitive will have knowing that is beyond the physical world. Many people who are spiritually intuitive are reported to have cried a lot as babies, as if they were having a real sulk about being born.

One of my students, Anisha, has just such a spiritual intuitive global reach. She feels everything from the depletion of the rainforests to the coral decaying in the ocean. She can't even put meat into her auric field and would rather cross the road than pass by a deli window display. Typically these intuitives are drawn to sacred areas of the world such as Glastonbury in the UK or Sedona in the USA. Anisha senses that everything is alive, from trees and plants to rocks. She also has an awareness of unseen energies and talks about spirits, nature spirits, and angels. She finds it difficult to focus on everyday subjects, but with practice she has developed her other four intuitive disciplines. In doing so, she has found that the physical world is full of love and joy. It isn't to be missed in favor of being in spirit more than in the physical body.

. . . .

For the purpose of understanding the types of intuition, that's really all you need to know. If you are interested in finding out more about the different intuitive types then you might find it helpful to read *Discover Your Psychic Type* by Sherrie Dillard (Llewellyn Publications, 2008). For now, let's look in detail at the four types of intuition and how they work...

Mental intuition: how the brain works with intuitive information

Your brain is amazing. It can write e-mails and listen to music at the same time. This is because there is a distinct difference between its left and right hemispheres, the two sides functioning independently yet in harmony with each other. It is important to say that the brain is incredible and that we don't fully understand it. For example, a person who has suffered an injury to the brain may find other parts of the brain developing to compensate for the loss. Now, I am not a neuroscientist – simply an avid brain enthusiast, I think everyone should have one!

The following explanation is simplified, but the left hemisphere is considered dominant, as it is the center of language and logic. The right hemisphere is non-verbal: working outside of time and space, creating mental images, clairvoyance, and is the source of your imagination. The left side perceives information in steps and pieces whereas the right perceives it as a whole.

For example something as simple as buying a motorcycle highlights the differences in how your life is affected, depending on whether you are predominantly a right- or left-brained thinker. A predominantly left-brain thinker appreciates the mechanics and performance of the motorcycle, whereas a right-brained thinker is more influenced by the shape, color, and overall beauty of the machine. The left hemisphere sees the motorcycle in parts; the right brain sees it as a whole.

The right hemisphere of the brain lacks language, so it communicates by sending a picture to the left hemisphere, which interprets the parts and puts them into words. The right hemisphere also communicates directly with our bodies using physical sensations and emotions. Most intuitive information stems from the right hemisphere of the brain, which then sends it over to the left hemisphere via the corpus callosum to translate and communicate it. This movement from right to left for communication means that some of the information is subject to misinterpretation.

This misunderstanding of information between the right and left hemispheres of the brain can be the reason why tests undertaken by parapsychology researchers are often unsuccessful. Psy information is received in the right hemisphere, but science requires it to be tested in a left-brained manner. You can't test the right hemisphere with a left-hemisphere approach – it's… well… illogical. However, for our purposes, it might help you to think of it as 'my rational, logical mind thinks this way, and my intuitive mind sees it that way.'

In the following table I've briefly outlined the different functions of the left and right brain. A quick look at each column will tell you whether you are predominantly a left- or right-brained thinker.

Left brain functions	Right brain functions
Uses logic	Uses feeling
Detail oriented	Big-picture oriented
Facts rule	Imagination rules
Words and language	Symbols and images
Present and past	Present and future
Maths and science	Philosophy and spirituality/religion
Can comprehend	Can 'get it' (i.e. meaning)
Knows	Believes
Acknowledges	Appreciates
Order/pattern perception	Spatial perception
Knows object's name	Knows object's function
Reality based	Fantasy based
Forms strategies	Presents possibilities
Practical	Impetuous
Safe	Risk taking

Our inner knowing has so much information to offer us about who we are and the world around us, but the left hemisphere of our brain is far too busy to allow it to come to our conscious attention. People don't believe that they are intuitive because they simply cannot put their inner knowing into words while the left hemisphere of their brain is so busy thinking about the past or making plans. As we all have a right hemisphere of the brain, the possibility exists for all of us to change our mode of thinking, listen to our world, and become more intuitive. To get in touch with your intuition you need to move from left-hemisphere thinking, the 'I' ego voice, to right-hemisphere, inner-knowing, big-picture thinking.

How to know when you're hearing the right brain

You are using your right brain if:

- You have ever found yourself talking to someone else in a flow of consciousness and, at the end, can't really remember what you said, but the other person is massively grateful for your helpful insight.

- You often think in pictures just when you start to fall asleep. A common occurrence is to play a movie-like sequence of images showing the events of the day.

- You have those pop-up memories from your past that seem unlinked to your current moment. They might be pictures from your past, perhaps not even interesting ones, but something as simple as a journey to the post office. You might even think of someone you haven't thought about for years.

- You make pop videos in your head while listening to music; I personally love doing that.

If any of these sound like you then you know what it is like to be predominantly a right-brain thinker, although some of these examples will be true of left-brain thinkers, too (because we all need both halves of our brain to operate). However, if you are predominantly a left-brain thinker and want to be more in the right hemisphere, I suggest giving your left hemisphere a vacation by thinking less in words. Enjoy daydreaming, dance, listen to music, sing, get some paint and make patterns with color, visualize your thoughts as if they were pictures running like a mind movie.

You can also use the world around you to help move you into a more right-brain way of being: take note and become curious about the patterns and shapes in cloud formations; allow advertising to bounce a totally different message to you by looking at the picture as a whole, taking note of which parts stand out, and becoming curious as to why; allow the world to become a colorful cartoon-like place that is telling a story beyond getting from A to B in the quickest time. This is how the right brain sees the world and by choosing to play with what we think of as 'reality' in this way, you can even become awakened to a different state of awareness.

Right brain takes over

I was asked a question by a man in the audience when I was giving a talk on mental intuition. He was a teacher of NLP (neuro-linguistic programming), and couldn't understand *how* after giving a class or lecture he couldn't do simple tasks, such as disconnecting his laptop from the projector or writing down his name and phone number. This is a classic example of someone who has moved his or her awareness into the right hemisphere of the brain. As we talked he understood that coming up with creative ideas for his students and reaching out for inspiration were all right-brained skills. He realized that it just took a while for him to come back into his usual mode after giving a talk.

Trusting mental intuition

You might hear a mental intuitive say 'I just know; I don't know how I know, I just know.' It is a knowing that hasn't gone through the critical analysis of the left brain; yet the feeling of strength and determination behind the knowing can be just as certain.

Inner knowing

At the height of my career in London, as I told you earlier, I just knew that I had to move to San Francisco for a while. On paper this was a crazy decision and many people tried to talk me out of it. As this was a kind of knowing that you can't explain, you can't argue with the logic of people who care about your wellbeing. The people who care can get very upset when you won't listen to logic or reason. Even if they do trust you, they can find it hard to trust the world itself – as if only bad people live beyond your doorstep. It might have been a 'crazy decision' but my years in San Francisco fulfilled me in more ways than I knew I was empty. How this knowing that 'I *have* to move there' came to me was like a download of information into my mental hard drive. I knew something was emerging out of me, as the inner knowing would come out in conversation with friends. Every question I needed an answer to in my life was greeted with a clairvoyant vision of the Golden Gate Bridge. Even the songs I heard on the radio had lines about San Francisco. And just how many reruns of *Charmed* can be shown on TV?

Of course, for the really big stuff, such as moving to another country, intuitive knowing is relatively easy – it is following it up with action that's more difficult. For smaller, but often equally as important, decisions the intuition may seem lighter and therefore more easily overlooked. Taking two minutes out of your day to silence the left hemisphere of the brain allows you to hear the download. Hence the expression to 'sleep on it' because when the left hemisphere is shut down for the evening the right hemisphere is still downloading. Once the download is complete, we might then see it as a clairvoyant vision. Of course, meditation (focus on the breath), walking, running, or anything that requires the left brain to focus on something that is repetitive will allow the right brain to come forward more. Even something as simple as washing the dishes means that while the left brain is in action, the right brain is in expansion. You might remember in the movie *Karate Kid* when the kung fu master got his apprentice to polish cars by putting 'wax on' and 'wax off' in a circle motion; focusing the mind on a seemingly 'meaningless' task helps open the right hemisphere of the mind.

Clairvoyance means 'clear seeing' but has come to mean 'seeing the future.' In this book, I am using it in its original sense. However, it is not often as clear as we would like. You might see an image of something from your life and discount it as your imagination. You only have the filing cabinet of your experience from which your intuition can draw images, but your imagination can create images from parts of things it has experienced and merge them together. Our imagination is not some childish fancy that has no meaning. Everything manmade you see around you started in someone's imagination. The imagination is how we create things. Imagination is the movie screen that clairvoyance plays upon. Even if you can't tell if something is imagination or intuition, don't give the imagination less importance than your intuition. Imagination is without logic and yet it can solve problems, or in the words of Albert Einstein:

> *'Imagination is more important than knowledge. For knowledge is limited to all we now know and understand, while imagination embraces the entire world, and all there ever will be to know and understand.'*

Clairvoyance through the imagination is a way to put the intuitive download into focus, without putting it through the doubting Thomas of your ego, which we will move on to later.

Clairaudience (clear hearing) is when we have formed the download into words, which means it won't be as 'pure' as knowing without words, but we must still engage with this intuitive knowing. It might be that we need to look for some backup information. We might find this by recognizing coincidences in the world, or use other intuitive methods to be sure of what we know.

Some people believe that clairaudience is their guide talking to them, some that it is their higher consciousness. If it has words, then the information has been parsed by the left hemisphere of your brain and therefore is less trustworthy. However, if you've ever had a situation where you say something and then wonder where that information came from (because you didn't think it first) then that can happen when you access a download. You can have intuitive downloads for other people in conversation, too. You can be talking and hearing yourself 'talk think' and might say

'That's brilliant, why didn't I think of that?' You can also find that in talking through one of your own issues with someone else, you suddenly come up with the solution to your problem. You say it aloud and, upon hearing yourself say it, understand it without having thought it before saying it. It is a remarkable way to be a reflective mirror and a great help to other people and yourself.

The most important idea to understand from all of this is to know that we don't use the whole of our brain's capacity, yet we seem stuck in the belief that the only answers worth having are those we go out and find by logic. Actually, the answers often lie somewhere beyond thinking: perhaps in a part of our consciousness that we are just beginning to connect with – our naked self, which isn't disguised by our ego. We'll get onto this in more detail in later chapters, but for now start thinking about giving your 'intuitive knowing' some space away from the thoughts in your head and allowing it to simply emerge and be heard.

Knowing beyond education

When we are children we are praised for performing mental skills, such as remembering multiplication tables or solving logic problems. These are skills that can be measured by tests, exams, and money in better careers. Unfortunately, there isn't an exam in common sense because it is not something you can measure. That is until you employ someone with no common sense and then you can measure its absence in financial loss and chaos.

It is also true that intuition can't be measured. Yet some of the most successful businesses started with a hunch or an intuitive insight for an idea or investment. At school we are taught a narrow band of knowledge that requires specific answers to specific questions, and we are rewarded for figuring out the correct solution. We aren't encouraged to value our gut instincts, as they simply don't reap the same rewards in attention and praise from teachers. In addition, if you can do mathematics by seeing patterns in numbers or you can talk about emotional reasons behind an author's words, you are more likely to cause alarm in the classroom than be rewarded for your skillful insights.

Number one connection

When I was a child, my mathematics teacher asked to see my 'workings out' at the side of the page. When I explained that I could see the patterns in the numbers, as they turned white and jumped up from the page, he seemed alarmed. He insisted that I must have 'workings out,' so he could see how I came to my answers. I got annoyed and insisted 'I am telling you how I find my answers.' He got even more annoyed and said 'That's NOT POSSIBLE!' So for the next few years I cheated and copied my friend's work, and failed my maths exam. That was until I studied 'mathematical archetypes of nature, art, and science' as part of my degree at the California Institute of Integral Studies. Then the patterns came back and this time I fell in love with the subject and understood the point of it.

People learn in different ways, but if you don't fit the conventional mold, then your intuitive knowing will be shut down by disapproval. Luckily mine wasn't, I just became introverted at school, while keeping all of my intuition open.

Somatic intuition: physical awareness

Most people these days have a basic awareness of their anatomy, physiology, and how to look after themselves with a healthy diet and exercise. Most also understand that there are many overlapping physical systems in operation within the body. Assuming full health and ability, you also have a complex sensory system – sight, touch, hearing, smell, and taste – which takes in information from the world around you, and is as important as your physical system. The nervous system controls and monitors all these systems, all wired up to a central computer – the brain, which works to maintain and preserve life. It therefore automatically oversees all the body's many functions and organizes everything at a cellular and energetic level. It is self-repairing and self-maintaining, leaving you free to get on with whatever it is you choose to do with your life. As you can see, you are quite amazing and the body is more than a tool by which we move through life, it is intelligent!

Much of what goes on around us the brain filters out because it believes it isn't important or useful. Of course, if we didn't have a filtering mechanism we would be constantly bombarded by millions of bits of information, so it is *how* our filtering system works that becomes the issue here.

Physical awareness

I was shown different photos of the inside of my stomach during a hospital exam. Not having a clue what I was looking at, I was able to see the different personalities or sound vibrations of each part of my stomach. I pointed at one photo and said to the doctor 'that one isn't happy.' He was surprised I could identify the one that had a problem as all the others were normal.

To some extent you are your body and your body is you. Yet all the different parts of your body have their own 'selves.' They all make their own unique sound. You are a biochemical and electromagnetic energy system. In fact you are a system of systems working together. All these systems are interdependent and can affect each other greatly. You also have subtler bodies, which exist in the same space as the physical body, but at different levels of vibration. You are a Russian doll made up of different levels within one another, each one reflecting and corresponding with the levels above and below it in the overall structure. These subtle bodies cannot be seen because they are composed of energy vibrating at frequencies outside of our normal range of perception.

Your energy centers and auric field are sensitive to the *sounds* of the world's energy all around you. Some of this information is useful to us; some of it is commonplace as it is part of our natural environment. We are surrounded by information. The physical body acts as a storehouse, holding information such as our DNA in its cells. It also holds information about the country we come from, the food we eat, and the family into which we were born. All of these various parts of information go together to make each 'you' have its own sound, which collectively becomes your unique theme tune and can be read intuitively by others and understood by you.

Your body is a walking radio capable of picking up intuitive information. The body in many different ways is both the receiver and processor of intuition. So your mental, emotional, and spiritual intuition may all be played out somatically. Those messages not understood by you (or filtered out by your perceptions as being not 'useful') can be stored in the body.

The body also stores emotional memories; echoes of things we didn't allow ourselves to feel or deal with at the time. All of this also has a sound quality to it. You might not be able to hear it, but you can feel it when you are not in harmony with yourself. As part of the human condition, we spend most of the time in the functional left hemisphere of the brain. In so doing we fail to acknowledge intuitive information received by the right hemisphere, which when ignored is stored in the body. When I treat clients, I can perceive/hear these hidden feelings or issues by touching or tuning in to a person's physical ailment. For example, a persistent problem with a tight muscle may originate in an ignored emotional issue or event that is causing the muscle to behave in this manner.

To unlock the intuitive messages stored in the body you might like to dance, have a massage, swim, or take part in any exercise or physical activity that doesn't require mental concentration, enabling you to release intuitive information to your body.

Tuning in to your body

The starting point in somatic intuition is to know what your body usually feels like. This doesn't mean that you have to run your hands over all of your lumps and bumps, but just to take note of what it feels like to be you. For example, when you are moving around the house doing some odd jobs, you will feel one way. Put some music on and it will change the sound of your body. It might mean you move differently around the house. It might change your emotions even, but the focus here is the body. Now let's change the circumstance – you're watching TV and a disturbing image flashes on the screen; your body goes tense. These are all ways to simply acknowledge how your body acts to outside stimuli. Now if you get some intuitive information, the body will respond accordingly, but without the outside influence. You might not notice the change, but the more you know your body the more aware you will become of its state.

Recognizing physical danger

When walking with a friend I have been known to direct them to cross the street with me, when we are already on the right side of the road for our destination. My friend starts to tell me we were on the right side already when a car takes the corner too sharply and would probably have hit us on the bend. When you work with somatic intuition, your body just moves. Not only out of danger, but toward the places and people that will give you the most benefit.

Emotional intuition: empaths and empathy

UK psychic Billy Roberts has a great exercise for seeing how energy can work. He says that if you were to take pips from an apple and leave them to dry overnight, then cut open a fresh apple and remove the pips, then place both sets of pips about an inch apart on white paper and relax your eyes, you would see two remarkable things: a ring of white energy around the fresh apple pips, and a line of energy form between the dry pips and the fresh pips. The fresh pips are reaching out and giving energy to the dry pips.

I believe that all living things are biologically programmed to heal other living things that are the same as themselves. On an energetic level we are all one and somehow we know this inside our energy system. There is a common occurrence that illustrates the gift of energy transference. If you have ever had a conversation with someone who is feeling sad or depressed, you may find yourself feeling tired while he or she may feel better. People say things like, 'I always feel so much better after talking to you.' Likewise, if you have ever gone to visit a friend in hospital, you might also have a feeling of being drained. This is because we automatically send energy to people who need it; empaths do this more than most.

Often people say that they feel drained around certain types of emotionally needy people. Those people can inspire us to move back from them as we feel this kind of tug in ourselves, a conflict of not wanting to 'give' but feeling that we might be forced to. These people can be described as being energy 'vampires' or people who are 'dark.' The truth is no one takes anything from us that we don't choose to give. We might not know that we are choosing to give it, but – just like the apple pips – we give and keep on giving until we set an intention not to any more.

Many of the disciplines that inspire people to put up walls of protection, using practices such as bathing in white light or visualizing psychic mirrors, don't work in my opinion; they are approaches that often create more negative energy than protect the person from their perception of an energy leech. How? For the simple reason that focusing on negative energy means you give it your attention rather than radiating positive energy toward other more positive things, which deserve your attention.

Love is the great protector: you choose to love yourself more than the person who is draining your energy; or you choose how much energy you wish to give them. The power of intention is remarkable, so to *intend* simply not to give out your energy helps. This is how many of the 'psychic protection' tools work. It is the intention that works, not the naked dancing. I'm sorry to inform you but you might be drawing symbols, dancing naked in the moonlight, turning round three times, and spitting, which all seem like a lot of hassle when setting out a clear intention is enough.

In my experience this is how many talismans and even curses work. You have to *believe in them* for them to work. These practices tap into the power of your intention, which is directly linked to the 'law of attraction,' otherwise known as manifestation.

Psychic what?

> I once heard a lady tell an audience to print and laminate a yin-yang symbol then cut it out, put it on their chair at work, and sit on it. This would block negative energy from a work colleague. Apart from making you look like a raving lunatic and therefore likely to give the person who doesn't like you cause not to like you, it also doesn't work.

. . . .

Self-love and acceptance are your greatest tools for protection. If someone's view of you doesn't resonate with your own, it simply becomes an opinion. I spent too long trying to please other people and never feeling like I was enough, only to find when I stopped, I made them happy just by being me.

What happens to an emotional intuitive is not just that they give out an abundance of energy, but they absorb that energy, too. Empaths pick up energy from other people and the world around them. Often they find themselves overwhelmed by feelings, which they have no logical reason for having. These emotions may come from reading their environment or from a person with whom they're physically close. Picking up energy like this can have a negative effect on their health as they may feel as if they are on an emotional rollercoaster. This overwhelming emotional state doesn't happen with all emotional intuitives, but there are some causes that allow this to take place.

The first cause is the solar plexus chakra being overactive. The solar plexus is located four fingers below your belly button and can scan a person to see if they are any danger to you. It brings back emotional information to this area and people describe this as having a 'gut' instinct. The problem comes when the solar plexus is scanning everyone and everything for danger. It can even give a feeling of *déjà vu* as it jumps forward in time to check nothing nasty is around the next corner. A person who doesn't feel safe in the world can end up having an overactive solar plexus. They may have experienced trauma or been taught from an early age that the world is an unsafe place. The solar plexus then adds to this problem by only bringing back negative information, thus continuing a cycle of mistrust. The emotional intuitive may then block their intuition in order not to hear any more bad news.

In reality, however, the world is full of love and an emotional intuitive has an amazing gift to be able to tune in to that world, and have the capacity to point out love to everyone who looks into the face of fear every day of their lives. Often those emotional intuitives who are trained to see love everywhere are dismissed and derided by those with an attitude of, 'life just isn't like that.' Openhearted emotional intuitives are hard to find; in fact, I think I have only met one. She worked as a dancer on a cruise ship. At the end of the contract she had hundreds of passenger e-mails; people she had adopted as friends. She wore bright colors and never let anything get her down. Her dancing was a joy to watch, but sadly the rest of the company found her *joie de vivre* more nauseating then the movement of the ship and often bullied her.

All an emotional intuitive needs is a sense of balance, self-belief, and grounding. These three things will turn what can be a curse into a unique blessing. Often an emotional intuitive is great at reading energy from objects using psychometry. They can also feel more beauty in people and have the vantage point of seeing past a person's ego into their loving soul. It is all a matter of perception and choosing what you tune in to. Allow love to be your driving force.

Your intuition and your emotions

We often use words that describe emotions in order to describe intuitive knowing, for example, 'I had a gut feeling' could be a good or a bad feeling. Yet we also use emotions to identify and describe how we are feeling at a given moment. We can make the distinction between the emotion and the feelings themselves – the literal sensations within the body, which we associate with particular emotional states. When we detect and identify the feeling, it becomes an emotion: an identified feeling. What has happened energetically is that the perception of an outside event causes an energetic response in the emotional body. When this response is powerful enough, it will be experienced as a sensation in the physical body due to the law of resonance (more on this in chapter 8). The body then produces chemical signals that correspond to the emotion, and these chemical signals carry the emotional energy into every cell in the body.

There are many things that can trigger an emotional response. Primarily, our mood will be determined not so much by what happens to us, as by the way we *perceive* what happens to us (i.e. our thoughts and what we tell ourselves about our situation). The body itself will also affect our mood. Emotions are experienced in the body: fear may manifest as a nauseous feeling in the pit of the stomach; sadness may be felt around the heart center and around the eyes; and anger in the arms and legs. This means that sometimes we can change how we are feeling simply by adjusting our breathing and posture.

Emotions are messages. They are a communication between our body and our spirit, with our mind as the mediator. Emotions may arise directly from the body, from past experiences, from our beliefs, or from deep within what we call the subconscious – which causes a problem when it comes to using emotions as an intuitive messenger. Your emotions are more likely to come from past experience than from your intuition. For example, you might have a negative feeling about a person because they remind you of someone from your past who acted badly toward you. Often adult education teachers come across this from students. The student will take a dislike to the teacher with no justifiable cause. This might make the teacher react by drawing away from that student or even disliking them. If the student is reacting from old pain experienced in childhood, the teacher will accidentally become an actor in the student's story about 'mean teachers.' If the teacher can see intuitively where the actions of the student are coming from, they have the chance to break the pattern and even heal the pain of the past. The student is reacting to the teacher as part of a system, nothing to do with the teacher as a person.

However, it's an amazing gift to be able to change someone's perspective. You can only do this if you can put your feelings to one side long enough to become curious about *why* the person is attacking you. When we understand a person's driving force, we can then change the situation's perspective with our actions. However, I would never suggest telling the person your intuitive insights, as they are unlikely to be conscious of acting negatively in the first place. All you can do is love them more fully and strongly. It can be a little exhausting but when it works, the rewards are far greater for both you and the other person. Only with intuitive loving and listening can we make these transformations.

So you can't trust your negative emotions as intuitive guides. In fact, intuition really only works well with the emotion of love; good feelings make better intuitive messengers than bad ones. So next time you have a bad feeling about something, become intuitively curious about it – see if you can intuitively identify a psychological cause rather than an intuitive warning.

Spiritual intuition: everything is energy

As the white feather floats down from the sky, the spiritual intuitive has their answer, but has forgotten the question. Spiritual intuition isn't based in the physical world. You might even wonder if it is based on this planet, as people who are deeply intuitive through their spiritual self can find communicating difficult. They often conform to the image of the new-age hippy; they find beauty in everything, but find being human difficult. They will often confess to communication with angels or ascended masters.

A spiritual intuitive who lives more in energy than in the body often finds everyday living a challenge. They may suffer feelings of being homesick even when they *are* home. Their intuitive skill is being able to see the big picture, but they can't always link it with a physical world of action. Their level of spirituality means that they just can't comprehend the human ego and are often hurt by the ego in others. They have strong links to other energy beings, the collective consciousness, and the Earth itself. They would have so much to teach those of us who are more grounded, if only they could make connections with the physical world. A spiritual intuitive will sense the world rather than feel it. The ability to sense comes from the aura and the chakras.

We have already touched upon the subject of the body's energy, but let's look at it a little more closely. Sometimes people claim that they can see the aura; however, the aura cannot ordinarily be seen with your eyes. What we physically see is possibly light as it bounces off solid objects; the aura is energy and not solid. In fact, your eyes see the world as if it were upside down. The image formed on the retina in our eye is an inverted one and our remarkable brain turns the image around for us to make sense of it, in much the same way that we have two eyes, but don't see two images.

People who can see the aura are probably in fact sensing it so strongly that the brain has added the missing details into the person's sight. In other words, the brain decides what we see. Right now, sitting in front of you, there might be a little green man from the planet Zog. If your brain cannot conceive of that little green man, however, your brain will simply take him out of the picture you have in your mind.

It was reported by Captain Cook and many of the other early sailors who visited remote islands in large ships, that the people on the islands couldn't see the ships. Their minds couldn't conceive of something so large sailing on water, and so blocked it out. This could also be why some people see the spirit of a dead person; their perception is so strong that it puts that image in place. This might be because they sense the dead person so strongly that the brain generates the clairvoyant image to match it. What you then have is a medium who will state, 'Your grandmother is standing beside you.' A wonderful gift if you are truly sensing a spirit. A not so wonderful one if you are picking up psychic information from the person you are talking to about their dead grandmother, and using that to allow the brain to fill in the blanks and not the grandmother at all. Personally, I believe it is really important to know all the possible variables before we make a fixed decision on something. Intuitive curiosity rather than purely believing what we are told is the best way to really understand the world.

With this in mind, become curious about your aura. You don't need to 'understand' the aura; you simply need to know it. Know what it feels like to be in your energy on a good day; know how it feels on a bad day. The aura has an abundance of energy and so, even if you can't see it, you can still sense and feel it. Enjoy it, play with it, know it is a valuable tool to give you intuitive information, and then forget about it. The aura looks after itself. As long as you look after your body, your aura will be fine.

The chakras

We can't have a conversation about the energy of the aura without mentioning the chakras. The chakras are centers of energy, located on the midline of the body. They supply much of the color and energy of the aura. The word chakra comes from Sanskrit and means 'wheel.' There are seven main chakras and each has a color and tone associated with it.

Point	Chakra	Color	Tone	Description
1	Root	Red	C	Being physically present and feeling at home in situations
2	Sacral	Orange	D	Feelings and emotions
3	Solar Plexus	Yellow	E	Works with ego intuition to assess if a person or situation is safe
4	Heart	Green	G	Love, kindness, and affection
5	Throat	Blue	B	Self-expression and speaking
6	Third Eye	Indigo	A	Insight and visualization; it is connected to the pineal gland, which is associated with clairvoyance
7	Crown	Violet	C♯	Wisdom and being at one with the world

There is also an eighth chakra, which is coming more to attention now as it is waking up more of our human potential. Its connections are to unconditional trust, intuitive knowing, and insight. The eighth chakra is the *transpersonal* point, which is becoming stronger as humanity realizes that it can't go on into the future with the same model of thinking as in the past.

As well as the seven main chakras, there are numerous minor chakras, such as those on the hands and feet. Invisible energy lines known as energy meridians run throughout the body, and connect all the chakras. When the subtle energy levels of the chakras are in harmony, the physical body maintains equilibrium and a positive relationship with the mental, emotional, and spiritual bodies.

Choose your energy

I have encountered many people who worry about closed chakras, unbalanced auras, psychic attack, energy draining, and the attachment of entities to the point where they can even stop getting on with their lives because of their anxiety about it. I worked with intuition and energy my whole life before these people alerted me to the potential dangers. I was perfectly fine until I knew all these dangers and then I suffered every single one of them. Why? Because my happy-go-lucky got lost! Fear brings you into vibrational alignment with the thing you fear, thus creating it. Love, joy, wonder, and curiosity are the greatest healing tools. When you feel yourself to be out of alignment, the only thing you are out of alignment with is love. The more you worry and try to fix it, the less love you are creating and the bigger the problem becomes. A bad thing happening to a good person is a part of reality. What makes it 'bad' is the definition and not the situation.

Your aura and energy system is extraordinary, too; it tells you all the time how aligned you are with love. When we intuitively hear our energy in terms of sound, we can hear if we are out of balance and we can then adjust our lifestyle accordingly. But the best way to make the adjustment is to do something fun: watch a comedy, go dancing, phone a friend, get a massage, play with a dog, eat a bag of chips. I honestly don't think it matters how you have a good time, but bring yourself out of worry by being as silly as you can. My favorite is musicals therapy: I put on a song and give my neighbors a reason to believe that *The X Factor* is quality TV. I sing my little heart out and no one swings round on a chair and says 'I want you.' I feel much better after. However, if you want to try this at home avoid singing anything from *Les Misérables;* at the end of the day, they always die.

Your body is a finely tuned instrument and the aura and chakras are a part of that fantastic and wondrous being that is you. A spiritual intuitive, over time, can learn to use their energy and become in tune with the energy of the world.

TUNING IN TO WHAT YOU KNOW

- There are four intuitive types: mental, emotional, somatic, and spiritual. You might have all of these types of intuitive knowing at your disposal; and you might be stronger in some areas than in others. The main thing is not to worry about it or hang your hat on being one or the other. From time to time all of them will be of use to you. Being a balanced person is far better than having an amazing intuitive skill in one direction; that way you can be open to them all.

Chapter 2
WHAT IS INTUITION AND WHY DO YOU NEED IT?

In the many years that I have been teaching intuition I felt something was missing. So I used my intuition to find out what it was. I always thought that there was one form of intuition to tune in to love or fear depending on how you see life, as a glass-half-full or a glass-half-empty person. However, if you understand that we live in a dualistic world of opposites – war/peace, affluence/poverty, etc. – you can see that there are also two polarities of intuition: love is at one end of the sound spectrum and fear is at the other. One form serves the ego and the other serves love. One has a high pitch (love) and one has a low pitch (fear). Ego-based intuition looks to keep you protected; it makes decisions through the filter of the ego, which also means any psychological baggage that you may be carrying will be added into the filter of your intuition. Perhaps this is why many people don't feel safe trusting their intuition; they are listening to the wrong form of knowing. When you listen to love it has no words, but it knows profoundly. It speaks of joy and resolution; it moves past fear toward love.

Gut versus heart instinct

Ego intuition is also known as a 'gut instinct.' Knowing when something feels bad is a good thing, but avoiding situations or people without knowing 'why' is limiting. Living a life of self-protection isn't *really* living. But this is what we are programmed to do; the ego protects the physical body. The bottom three chakras connect to the body and protect it. The solar plexus reaches out from the body and reads people and/or situations. It then takes this information to the sacral chakra, which turns it into a feeling. The feeling is taken into the gut brain; yes there is a brain in your gut! Embedded in the line of the intestines is the enteric nervous system, with hundreds of millions of neurons – one-thousandth the number in your brain. This network is termed the second brain and controls the gut function. Gut neurons communicate with the brain through the vagus nerve, which runs from the base of the brain to the chest and abdomen. The clearest connection between the gut and the mind, this is how we experience anxiety and stress. We've all experienced those moments of fear or stress when your guts literally feel like they are churning or liquid.

One way of interpreting or understanding this mind–gut connection is through the chakras. Our solar plexus chakra picks up signals from people or situations and looks for them to be dangerous; a repeat of something that hurt us in our past, or simply is not in alignment with what we want. This information is then absorbed by the sacral chakra and turned into emotions. The gut brain then reads these emotions and sends this information for analysis by the brain, which tries to digest it logically by using words. In this way, you can see how our stomach is our understanding of what we are digesting from the outside world – not just in our food and water, but our emotions, too – which also goes some way to explaining why conditions such as coeliac disease and IBS (irritable bowel syndrome) are often linked to stress and anxiety.

Although gut instinct is very important, as discussed in the previous chapter it can lead to problems if we have a very active solar plexus. What makes the solar plexus active is our psychology; it is our belief in our capacity to feel safe in the world. If we don't trust ourselves to cope, or trust the world to be a good place, our solar plexus will be overactive and give us the intuitive heads-up on impending doom all the time. This can lead to feelings of anxiety and stress with no sign of a real cause. Often this is the case with empaths; they just become too sensitive. Rather than trying to change your chakras, which know far better than your ego, start to look at your psychology and the underlying causes of your stress, anxiety, and fears.

Resolving them could be as simple as making a list of every amazing thing you have ever done, of all the wonderful acts of human kindness you see. Start to unravel the belief that the world isn't safe, and build upon the positive belief in you. Developing your heart- or love-based intuition will also change the messages your gut is giving you, too. Unlike gut intuition, love-based intuition doesn't work on the development of the ego's belief in its problems and fears. Instead it shines a light into the only real truth there is... love.

Love-based intuition

When I work with a client I take their belief in their problems seriously, but I don't consider they have a problem. To me, some are in a holding pattern of unhappiness while they are waiting for more information. I give them that information so that they can move through the thing that is holding them in their ego. This way, between the two of us, we can bring more love into life. During the session, if I am not feeling love for the client I usually conclude the appointment.

Some people are not ready for that kind of love or breakthrough. This in no way means my consultations are fluffy; a kick up the backside can be just as loving as offering a hand to hold. But if I don't love them I know I had my ego filter on during the appointment. This means, for example, if I've had a bad relationship with a rock star ex-boyfriend, I might see bad things about my client's relationship with her fabulous rock star boyfriend. Ego intuition looks everywhere for information that might be useful. Love intuition simply listens for the sound resonance: is it in alignment or is it not? As the intuitive inquirer, you can then become curious about what you feel and receive more accurate information. The trick is to stay in the higher pitch of a loving resonance. Love expands, fear limits. We want to make decisions in life from the heart, not from the head.

Not how but why

All this is useful knowledge in becoming more intuitive but the main thing about intuition is not the *how*, but the *why*. Why do you want to use intuition? The purpose behind your intuition will also play a very large part in how strong your intuition becomes. The main reason most people want to use intuition is the avoidance of pain. You might think this is a limited perspective on the use of intuition but during my many years teaching intuition in London, I would interview students who wanted to develop their intuitive skills. I would start each interview by asking why they wanted to learn. Some would answer that they wanted to help others, but most would say they wanted to trust their intuition for decision-making.

In life people often feel they want to be on the 'right' path, heading in the 'right' direction, with the 'right' partner, job, etc. The belief that you are heading in the 'wrong' direction is a belief that 'it' will lead to pain and disappointment. What it often leads to is actually learning, as if life somehow knew better than we did and took us exactly where we needed to be; to learn what we needed to know. All the worry about the 'wrong' direction just made us unhappy. By trying to avoid pain, going around the mountain, it takes us longer to be living 'on purpose,' and what's more we are miserably worried while doing it. The avoidance of pain activates your fear-based intuitive knowing; you will then read the world to be a scary place. If you don't believe you can handle what life can throw at you, you will avoid living fully. And one thing I know for sure is life never gives you more than you can handle. You might need to learn some juggling tricks, but never so many balls that you drop them all.

It is fear that will usually drive someone to seek the guidance of a psychic. This can be boiled down to:

- The fear of losing what you have;

- Or the fear of not getting what you want.

Yet if pain is a necessary growth tool, you might find your intuition is being limited to small, imprisoning answers. Ego-based intuition seeks the avoidance of pain. Love-based intuition seeks growth and positive evolution. Love perceives pain as a growth tool or an emotional warning message and not as a negative thing to be avoided.

So now you know that intuition will not work well without the following three factors – purpose, love, and curiosity – being part of the reason that you are seeking answers.

Purpose

When we make decisions by thinking alone, we limit ourselves to ideas based on information that we already know. Intuition will guide us to make decisions with our heart and also step into a 'knowing' that isn't conscious. However, this intuitive guidance system only works if there is purpose. So you couldn't expect to be guided by simply thinking, 'What should I do with my life?' The emerging desire behind the question might be:

- How can I lead a creative life?

- How can my life be of the best use for others?

- How can I have a happy, fulfilled existence?

Simply adding purpose to a day can also create more intuitive knowing throughout that day.

Purpose could also be described as 'intention,' which we discussed briefly in the previous chapter. Setting out what you want from a day, a week, or even a year gives your inner guidance system a focus with which to work. Use your imagination, step into wonder, and create purpose from a space of being excited.

Knowing what you want

When learning intuition in a classroom, many students will practice giving readings to each other. Unless the seeker has a purpose behind the reading, the intuitive information is weak. At the start of all of my consultations, I always ask my clients, 'What do you want to get out of this session?' If they didn't originally come with an intention, it gets them to think about a purpose and makes the session stronger.

Being as famous as I am as an intuitive (please, lower your eyebrows) I find many clients come to see me without a purpose, just to see what I have to say. But if you haven't got much going on in your life then there won't be much to see. For example, a client raved about me to her friend (in a good way, of course) and so her friend came to see me and wanted amazing insights into her rather uninteresting life. I'm not being mean here, but I wouldn't let them pay me for a service I can't provide. However, instructions for an amazing life are revealed upon the impact of my foot on a behind.

More seriously, it is worth just accepting that we all go through times when we are stable and not growing, just as the Earth goes into winter. Intuition for some people is about solving problems – that is what gives it purpose, and without that purpose, intuition doesn't work for them.

Living on purpose: the science bit

In any scientific study, any experiment needs to be repeatable for a large percentage of the tests, in order for the results to be accepted as 'proven.' Dr. Caroline Watt, a founder of the Koestler Parapsychology Unit research group in the Psychology Department of the University of Edinburgh has been conducting experiments on Psy energy, but including what I perceive to be the missing elements of 'love' and 'purpose.' To me, these are the most important elements in any test on right-brain ability.

In July 2008, Caroline courageously gave a talk at a meeting for the Society for Psychical Research. The audience was mainly composed of the Skeptics Society, who seemed to be mostly unhappy with Caroline's findings and discounted them as best as they could. In her lecture she described a scientific test in which a subject was asked to concentrate on the flame of a candle. In another room a person, we shall call the 'sender,' was given times at which they were to send help in the form of positive thoughts to the person trying to keep focused on the candle. It was found that when the sender transmitted energetic help, the person concentrating on the flame was able to focus more (even though they didn't know when this help was coming). Participants had a variety of different beliefs: those tested by believer experimenters showed the 'remote helping' effect; those tested by skeptical experimenters did not show any effect.

The same experiment was recreated by my students under less scientific conditions, and we discovered the same results. This indicates that when we create an energetic bond, we could say a bond of loving energy, there is intuition. Without this loving bond there is no intuition. I have found this with clients and, as I said earlier, I can honestly only work with clients where I can create this bond. I don't feel intuitively linked to people all the time. However, if I think of the wonder of creation and the beauty that can be found in all people and the love, my intuition opens to allow me to receive information once again.

Love

Often when we look for intuitive knowing it's because we are trying to avoid something going 'wrong.' What happens when we try and control life is that we step into the left hemisphere of the brain. This is the action mind; it calculates and works on logic. When this part of the brain is active, the intuitive mind in the right hemisphere of the brain is receiving information, but you can't hear it because the left hemisphere is busy in a state of concern or worry. If we take a moment to consider 'What would love say to this?' then we open the channels to be able to hear our intuitive knowing.

Of course, there are many ways in which we can 'hear.' This may come as a feeling in your body. So when you pose the question 'What would love say to this?' put your hand on your heart, so that you have a better connection with your body. The more we love in a day, the more our intuition works. This could be feeling a sense of love about anything: taking a moment to appreciate a flower or the first cup of coffee in the morning. Being present with a moment of love, appreciation, or gratitude heightens intuitive awareness. The practice of mindfulness can help enhance intuition. Mindfulness is developed by an attentive awareness to things in the present moment and is often used as a meditation tool, for example an attentive awareness and focus on the breath. When we are fully present with something, or someone, there is love. If you have ever tried to really look into another person's eyes you will feel a development of love between the two of you. Even with a perfect stranger. Without love there is no purpose for intuition and therefore there is no intuition. This is true, even if you are getting paid to be intuitive and you love money; there will still be no purpose for intuition. Intuition is a gift that cannot be bought; it can only be received, and its wrapping is love.

Having purpose and love behind your intuition means that your intuitive knowing becomes part of a self-development practice rather than an avoidance of pain. It makes you feel secure enough in yourself to make braver, more empowered decisions based in love and not fear. It also means that we can hear others more clearly when we become aware of the root cause of our needs.

Trusting your intuition

A question that comes up all the time in workshops and courses is, 'How can I tell the difference between my imagination and my intuition?' The answer to this question is really quite complex, as it isn't just imagination that gets in the way of your intuitive knowing – so let's break it down.

First, it's important to say that the imagination is a vital aspect of intuition. Imagination is formed in the right hemisphere of the brain, which is also the center of your intuition. In addition, your imagination is your tool for manifestation, so if you find yourself getting strong images, ideas, feelings, or thoughts then you need to pay them the same amount of attention. Whether imagination or intuition, you need to heed both.

In the scenario of reading or tuning in to another person, if what you are receiving feels different to your normal self then it is very rarely your imagination. You might get some meaning confused when you send the information from the non-verbal right hemisphere to the verbal left hemisphere of the brain, but it is unlikely that you are completely wrong. The way we explain things to another person in this context is so important. The person may not be able to accept being told that they have lots of 'problems,' but can understand that they have a lot of 'issues.' A subtle change of language can make all the difference. Choosing the right words is an intuitive art form that takes lots of practice.

Many people believe that what they receive through their intuitive clairvoyance is just their own mind because the images they are seeing are from their life. The truth is your life experience is all you have to create the tools you can use. If you were asked to picture a church, you might see one you know or one that is a combination of churches you have seen before. You might just see a cross, if this is the symbol of a church for you. It is unlikely, however, that you have designed a church in your mind from scratch, but people somehow think that they should see the exact church in relation to the person they are reading. That just isn't possible. This also depends on your intuitive type:

- Mental intuitives see a composite image of a church made up from ones they have seen before.

- Emotional intuitives feel happy (marriage in a church) or sad (graveyard).

- Spiritual intuitives won't have any connection: 'God is in the universe not in a building.'

- Somatic intuitives connect to the word 'church.'

So, as another example, if you wanted to talk about your friend's partner, your memory may present an image of your own partner, a family member, or another friend. It could be that this person shares the same personality trait, name, or characteristic.

Many people take the route of using tools such as tarot cards to access the intuitive mind. The image on the tarot card opens the right hemisphere of the brain. Regardless of what the card means by the definition in the guidebook, people relate to the character archetypes on the cards and downloads of intuitive knowing can be accessed. However, it is not the images on the cards that form the intuition, they are just a tool to access a talent that you already have in your imagination and memories. In fact, the world is one big tarot pack.

Curiosity

The third and final trick to finding the meaning behind your intuitive information is to become curious about it. If you were to put this curiosity into words you might say, 'Why am I seeing this?' However, avoid words if you can, as this will shift you from the non-verbal right hemisphere to the verbal left hemisphere. You simply need to think of the 'feeling' you get when you are curious – that is what you are looking for.

As you continue to be curious, often another wave of information comes through. You might have already voiced or acknowledged the first images or feelings and, as you do so, more information comes through to you. If you stay curious, more unfolds and your curiosity takes you deeper into the information. The energy becomes stronger, the curiosity becomes deeper, and love starts to flow.

This curiosity can make you feel like you are the observer of mankind. As you become more curious you feel more love, which lifts your vibration higher. If you are doing a reading for someone else, it then allows that you see much more of this person as you are lifted in vibration. It is the curiosity, the love, and the purpose to help heal that takes you to the depth of understanding. At this point you no longer have to worry about your imagination, as you are *connected*, almost as if you and the person you are reading are one, as you 'see' them with total compassion and understanding.

If you put your hand in water that is the same temperature as your hand, you will barely feel the water; yet if you are colder or hotter than the water the difference is more apparent. The same works with vibration. If you, as the intuitive, have a higher vibration, which is closer to love, the easier it is to see the complexities of the other person's vibration. This allows you to receive more intuitive knowledge, which directs you to the points in the person's life where any 'discord' first originated.

As part of your intuition, you will often receive flashbacks from your past, or flashes of your present along with information. Some can be memory replay, but it is the most vivid memories playing back that you need to take note of and heed. Intuition also comes during states of heightened awareness. I call this a 'cartoon state' as that's what it looks like. It is a moment in a day when you notice that your consciousness has shifted somehow. The world suddenly sharpens into focus, the colors are brighter, and the shapes are more 3D. Perhaps a conversation next to you becomes louder and they're talking about the very thing you were just thinking about; or the radio is playing 'that song' with the words you needed to hear. This state of heightened awareness is also known as one form of 'awakening' as you are fully in the present moment and less in the ego state of awareness.

Cartoon state

In one of my cartoon states, I was walking to my office off Pall Mall in Piccadilly where I'd been working on Thursdays for a while, and had a happy little routine for my 10am start. But today was different.

First, I was nearly hit by a bus (London buses take no prisoners). Then a man cleaning the street nearly hit me with a broom when he suddenly decided to wield it over his head as if he was dancing in *Mary Poppins*. I finally got to the big doors just as they closed in front of me (and had to press the buzzer to open them again). But none of this felt bad. In fact, I was intrigued, and started to look inward as I was curious about my cartoon state. I usually turn off my phone at the door but on that day, because of the bizarre events of the morning so far, intuitively I kept it on silent and next to me on the desk. I'm glad I did, because if I hadn't taken notice of the signs, I would have missed an incredibly important phone call.

. . . .

Curiosity + love + purpose = understanding

It is the curiosity, the love, and the purpose to help heal that takes you to the depths of understanding. From the way you look at advertising billboards, overhear someone's loud phone conversation, or notice patterns in the clouds; when you look at the world with curious eyes everything can have a strange sense of coincidence about it. It changes the world from being a place where you exist to a place that exists within you. When you look at the world through curious eyes you are able to be in unison with what really matters. You meet people who can aid you in your purpose, you find shortcuts you didn't know existed, and you feel part of everything. Simply put, life becomes less of a struggle and more of an intuitive flow in the right direction.

Predominantly, all intuitive information feels positive. You might be driving a car and have a positive feeling about turning left, rather than a bad feeling about going straight on; it is rare to have a bad feeling about the road ahead. If you ever examine an intuitive knowing after the event, you might say, 'I knew I shouldn't have done that.' But it doesn't mean the feeling was negative.

Positive intuition

A few years ago, when I worked on a cruise ship with a boyfriend, we stopped at a port in Namibia and had the chance to go quad biking in the desert. I was a bit of a girl racer in my youth and used to ride motorbikes and race old cars round a track, so usually I'd have jumped at the chance. But that day I felt really strongly that I wanted to explore in a 4×4 instead. The more my partner talked about the quad bikes, the more determined I felt that the 4×4 would be better. All I could tell him was that I 'had a bad feeling about the bikes.' Actually, this was not the case – I just had a positive feeling about the 4×4. Sadly, my intuition was correct and my boyfriend had an accident and broke his collarbone, which resulted in him being sent off the ship and the loss of his job. Sometimes, it's difficult not to say 'I told you so,' but it is also very difficult to wring your girlfriend's neck with one hand.

We are programmed to listen for the negative, so we rarely say, 'I have a great feeling about this.' The human ego is trying to protect the physical body, so it tends to look for the negative. Ego makes its decisions from fear; it needs everything to be kept limited. So if you have a fear about something, it's unlikely to be your intuition talking. So why doesn't intuition work with fear? Intuition works from a loving vibration, and is always trying to keep you in touch with love and your true potential. But when you are in the middle of feeling scared about something, it is hard to feel your intuition, as the positive loving vibration is having a hard time fighting though the fear.

Think of it this way: imagine that everything is made of chords of energy, like a harp. The truth of a situation can be felt as if it were sound. You know when everything is in harmony because it sounds and feels right. You can hear a clear sound with no discord. However, if the tuning changes, you can hear and sense the difference as everything becomes a little off key. You are still attuned to the chords, but something is off. This is very much how it sounds to an intuitive when someone lies, if something difficult has taken place in a space, or just when someone is feeling a little off color.

Now imagine that *you* are that harp: your emotions are the strings, you feel the vibrations of the world through the resonance. If your strings are not tuned correctly then you might think the world is out of tune, when in actual fact it is your emotions. This is the single biggest problem with intuitive knowing. If your emotional strings are being pulled and triggered, it becomes hard to know if you are having an intuitive reaction to something or if it is a past experience having an emotional repeat.

To overcome this, you need to simply trust yourself as the instrument that all the tunes of life are played upon. If you can trust *you* as an intuitive tool, you know all of your information is correct. However, it would be asking a lot to expect you to be emotionally in tune and balanced at all times. We are all learning and we all go out of balance from time to time. Even the Earth goes into winter, but as humans we expect to be always in a time of personal growth; springtime all the time. It's just not possible. The trick is to intuitively understand your seasons. It is okay to have a harmonizing wobble in life; you'll notice that the Earth also lets off the occasional volcano and earthquake, too. The trick is to intuitively know what you are listening for over the commotion of everyday existence. You are listening for the loving pitch: it feels a little like excitement or joy; it feels a little silly and childlike. That simply is what intuition feels like. It never feels heavy or bad. You know to trust your intuition when you can hear that gentle sound no matter what other discord is going on around it.

That might seem difficult, but now you have the explanation for what intuition feels like in words, I have no doubt that you will feel it more often.

A common cause for a drop in intuition

People always tell you that you have to think 'positive,' but when you're deep in the throes of feeling negative it is normally the last thing you want to hear. So, it might help to know that 'being' positive is just as important.

Imagine your mind has two floors and an elevator to move between them. Floor one is the neocortex, which makes all of your brilliant decisions: it is intuitive, inspired, and motivated. Then there is the basement, the reptilian brain (the affectionate term for the basal ganglia, but more on that later), which is in charge of keeping the body safe and reacts to hostile or frightening situations. Its normal way of dealing with fear can be well remembered using four Fs:

1. **Flight**: run away; get out of there.

2. **Fight**: stand still and I'll give you a bunch of fives in the shape of a fist.

3. **Freeze**: most animals and insects do this; they keep still and play dead or are paralyzed with fear.

4. **Food**: give the body energy to help it cope with the situation.

What's important here is to understand that we cannot be on both floors at the same time, which means that these parts of the brain are not active simultaneously. What activates the elevator to go up or down is not situations in your life, but how you feel about them emotionally. The emotions that correspond with your basement include:

- Boredom
- Pessimism
- Frustration
- Irritation
- Impatience
- Feeling overwhelmed
- Disappointment
- Doubt
- Worry
- Blame
- Discouragement
- Anger
- Revenge
- Hatred
- Rage
- Jealousy
- Insecurity
- Guilt

- Unworthiness
- Fear
- Grief
- Depression
- Despair
- Powerlessness

You can see why when you are in the grip of any of these emotions, it is impossible to see a way out, as you're on the wrong floor. The part of the brain that works out solutions isn't the one you're functioning from.

I remember if I fell into boredom as a child I would be told 'If you're bored go and do something,' but when you're bored you simply can't think. When you remember your school days, you might recall that in classes you weren't good at or were taught by a boring teacher, you just couldn't think. This is also an important point if you're being bullied (either at school or as an adult) because when you are unhappy or fearful you go into the basement of your mind, which delivers one of the four Fs: flight, fight, freeze, or food.

The mind, however, works with the body to make sure that we stay at floor one with an open and fully functioning mind. This is where you help the body out because before you hit the emotion of 'overwhelm' you can take some physical activity, which will enable your body to release serotonin (the happy hormone), which also makes you feel more relaxed, joyful, and produces a sense of wellbeing. There are lots of ways to do this: exercise, take time out for meditation, laugh, sing, dance, play with animals and children, or simply find some way to have fun and head back to the first floor.

We must *actively* switch our mind and look for the positive in a negative situation. In fact anything that makes you feel:

- Joy
- Empowerment
- Freedom
- Love
- Appreciation
- Passion
- Enthusiasm
- Eagerness
- Positive expectation
- Belief
- Optimism
- Hopefulness
- Contentment

These emotions all exist on the first floor.

Sleep

Every morning you are reborn; the elevator is reset to floor one as you wake up refreshed and ready. Your mind does this by dreaming. Anything that is still causing you stress at the end of the day will be worked through at night in your dreams. It explains why some mornings you still feel tired because you've had a night of unraveling in your dreams. Imagine your mind has a recycle can for every issue that you didn't deal with during the day. Some of these issues are yours, some other peoples, and some are from TV shows or the media – the subconscious mind can't always tell the difference. At night we sort through the recycling, process the useful stuff, and chuck out what we don't need. If there's a lot to process we might wake up, so we can go through the rest and not start the new day with it hanging over us. However, then what often happens is that we add to the can with thoughts of 'If I don't get some sleep, I'll be useless tomorrow' and then start panicking.

However, there is a school of thought that says we are meant to wake up partway through the night; that the best insights are at 3 a.m. If I wake up I often do something, perhaps write a blog, go to the bathroom, or even clean the house. Then I find that I fall asleep much more quickly without stressing about it. It is almost a sacred time, my time; I am not expected to do anything, no one needs me. Using that time to daydream in my mind in pictures about beautiful things I am grateful for often brings me back to sleep. You will really help yourself solve the problems of the day if you take some time to do some happy stuff or simply 'sleep on it.' You might also find that at around 3:30 to 4 p.m. you have a dip in energy and really want an afternoon nap. If you imagine that at 3:30 a.m. your masculine dynamic starts work preparing you for the day and stays with you working until 3:30 p.m. then your female dynamic comes and allows you to process all the emotions behind all of the work your male dynamic has been doing. This is the balance of doing and being.

Although I have to say that I do love a sleep in the afternoon; I call it spiritual research. Please see the above as permission for you to do the same. Just don't forget to pick up the kids from school.

Diet

If you're a nighttime thinker you might also want to take a look at your diet. More than two glasses of wine and you may find yourself waking up in the middle of the night with your heart beating fast and feelings of anxiety. There is a surprising amount of sugar in wine (and beer), and when your blood sugar drops rapidly it can cause you to wake up. Caffeine is a bit of an obvious culprit in preventing you from getting to sleep, so pay attention to what you are drinking in the afternoon. Heavy meals eaten late at night can be hard to digest and too much dairy can cause a buildup of mucus, which can lead to waking yourself up snoring… or being smothered by your partner.

As more is understood by medical science about having a brain in the gut, more links are drawn between our emotions and conditions such as IBS and feelings of anxiety (butterflies) in the stomach. Eating well and getting a great night's sleep are all part of looking after your intuition as well as your body. You only get one body, so taking time to look after it is the single most important part of your day. If you are overstressed, overworked, or overwhelmed then do everything in your power to change it or find help. Nothing is more important than being healthy and happy. And there is no such thing as a happy tomorrow if you're killing yourself for it today.

Staying on the first floor

Intuition, synchronicity, insights, awareness, and clarity are all on the first floor. When people tell me they have lost their intuition, they often don't realize it went at the same time that they stopped being happy. They look for intuition to give them a lead into happiness, but happiness leads them to intuition. There are two solutions to this: one is to listen for your intuition first thing in the morning before any fearful thoughts drop the elevator; the other is to find something that takes you out of a place of fear. I can't tell you what works for you, as you are unique, but I know if you're in that space you might find it difficult to think of it for yourself.

One answer is to look for it when you *are* happy, try and pay attention to what was going on to lead you there. Make a note of it so you have a reference should you one day lose yourself. I have a weekly practice, listed below, which keeps me on floor one and they are the four supports of my life:

1. I dance 'five rhythms' or 'ecstatic' dance on my own or with a group. I allow emotions to come up from my body and mind, anything I was too busy to realize at the time, and I dance them out.

2. I put on songs from musicals and I sing them as loud as I can with as many actions as possible. There is a phrase that I was taught at drama school by my friend Neil, and I have used it ever since – 'Musicals Therapy'.

3. I listen to the radio: I have spur-of-the-moment song and dance breakouts with all the moves. It could happen at any time and I do stop work to allow it.

4. I am nice to everyone when I first meet them; I make jokes and act a little eccentric. People might think I am a little crazy, and they're maybe more than a little right, but I am fighting for my sanity. But then perhaps it is the crazy people who think they are normal, the normal question whether they are crazy!

If I am communicating from floor one, I am in flow. I don't freeze, I don't fight, I don't run away, and I don't pig out on chips! Also there's a fifth 'F' (fornication) that is just the best for releasing the happy hormone when you're with the right person.

Happiness is like a beach ball in the water of your emotions. No matter how many of your thoughts try to hold it down, it will always float to the top. You don't have to think about happiness and how to make yourself happy; you just need to allow it to float to the top of your life, by giving it the time and space to do so. As Albert Einstein said, 'The only real valuable thing is intuition,' and developing love-based intuition will give you inner guidance for less fearful decision-making.

TUNING IN TO WHAT YOU KNOW

- Sometimes just accept that you are in a down phase and life is just ordinary; intuition is useless unless there is 'intention' behind it. The answer is to have purpose, love, and be curious. Staying present in the moment means you'll be less distracted by 'fear-based intuition' and be able to hear/receive love-based intuition more easily.

- Connected to this, you'll find it difficult to tune in to your love-based intuition when you are experiencing your basement emotions because you are operating from an ancient inbuilt part of your brain (the reptile brain), which utilizes the four Fs to keep you safe. All the four Fs are fear-based so you need to move from a state of fear to one of love.

- Find a weekly practice that keeps you on floor one. It could include anything that brings you up from the basement emotions and makes you feel happy.

Chapter 3
THE MOST REMARKABLE YOU

By now I hope that you have started to question yourself, your ego, and begun to wonder where all that fear came from? What gave birth to the ego and stopped us from tuning in to our latent intuition? Well, I have a theory about that...

Imagine that once you were the only thing that existed. You were completely indescribable because there was nothing to compare you to, and in order to get a grasp of how we looked we'll use a mirror as a metaphor for our story.

Once upon a time, before time began, there was an indescribably large mirror of light. The mirror (you) had a crazy thought, 'What if I could experience myself.' In order to experience what we are, we have to know what we are not, which creates a polarity of opposites. In the moment of this thought, which by the way was likely to be the one and only thought you'd ever had, the mirror shattered right in the center. This is known as the big bang. The first ripple of sound coming from the bang held the largest shards of glass. These shards were now separate and had their own consciousness; they could remember that they were once part of one big mirror. (If you're a spiritual intuitive you might know these shards to be angels or guides.)

Each ripple of sound, as it journeyed away from the mirror, became more solid until the memory of the mirror was completely lost. However, each shard still carried a feeling of longing and loneliness, which drove them to look for unity within each other. But the shards chose to experience what they are not, and this is why at times they felt so very alone. They would even communicate to each other from the dull side of the mirror, denying their connection to each other. It was too painful see themselves reflected back to each other. They called the dull side of the mirror 'ego' and the reflective side 'love.' It was impossible to look at their reflection in someone else's mirror and not remember that they were once part of a whole. But the decision to leave held such pain and guilt that they totally forgot about the big bang, and the broken mirror became just an idea, just a dream. It is impossible to leave yourself. As each shard of mirror was part of a whole, the break was an illusion. We are dreaming duality, but we never left home.

This is the idea of 'oneness' or 'nonduality.' Believing that we are living a dream doesn't matter so much for the understanding of this book. However, it does give us an entry point into a conversation about the ego and how it can prevent us from tuning in to our intuition – our essence.

A sense of purpose and belonging

I imagine that our hearts hold a piece of this divine mirror. When the dull side of the mirror is up, the heart feels empty. We then think that whatever we buy, have, do, or choose will make us feel full again. So we buy a new house, car, clothes, food; we study, change jobs, blame circumstance, and do our best to fill the empty hole in our hearts. In fact, this is often why advertising has such a strong effect on us: 'If you buy this thing, you will stop the emptiness.' We will do anything to give ourselves a sense of purpose and belonging. When we turn the mirror round and shine our love and reflective side out, we become open and realize that we have always been full. The hole in our heart acts like a lampshade for the love we have to give. Through this opening to love, we inspire others to shine their mirrored love out, too. If we all shone mirror-side out, the mirror would come back to being as one whole.

However we are in a self-imposed trap, and many people don't feel safe to shine their light; it feels vulnerable to be possibly the only light in the darkness. The dull side of the mirror is our ego; the reflective side of the mirror is our love. The ego is the ruler of our fear; so when fear wins, we simply don't shine.

The ego

Humans are profoundly intelligent. We have intelligent minds and bodies, and have brought about awe-inspiring creations. Everything manmade started in the imagination, and from that place we have brought into being the most terrifyingly destructive things to hurt the planet and everything on it, including us. Yet in our artistic imagination we create such beauty. No matter how intelligent we are, we coexist with an aspect of ourselves that is in itself insane. When you look back at our history, you see the evidence of human insanity. It is the part of us that says, 'What about me?'

Ego believes we are separate from other humans. Ego feels pain and loneliness; it feels desperation. Ego feels it isn't seen or heard enough. Ego believes its happiness lies somewhere in the future, in a sense of achievement or recognition. Ego believes it is right and clever, and that it can harm others for its own protection. However, before we all get depressed, we are coming to the end of this aspect of being human. Sadly, one way or another, we will shift our consciousness to see, think, and feel beyond this part of ourselves or else we will die out as a species. We are without a doubt at a tipping point in our consciousness. The way forward is to expand our consciousness into intuitive knowing.

In every human being there is the madness and the sanity. Awakening to be able to hear and be liberated is to intuitively know who you really are outside of the madness. The ego mind is always built on identification. We need to know beyond the 'I am,' 'my name is,' 'I am a man or a woman,' or even 'that is my house,' 'car,' 'wife,' 'husband.' We know we are much more than this, but often we simply don't know how to get in touch with that aspect of ourselves that is beyond the 'I am.' However, we cannot dismiss one half of ourself to reach the other. We can't be in denial of our insanity. The awakening is to know that we are insane and to deal with it in any positive way we can. Mindfulness, awareness, humor, gratitude, forgiveness, self-development – but the first part has to be the acknowledgment of what is ruling your decision in any given moment. Is it your ego or your intuitive knowing that is running your life?

Many people see removing the ego as the way to enlightenment, believing that it creates blocks to us finding divine love. The irony is that the desire to reach enlightenment comes from the ego. It can only be the ego that wishes to seek enlightenment, so in a sense the ego wishes to put us on a 'path' to find enlightenment, but then only allows us to seek, not to find. In our very center, we are already enlightened, so there is no path to find enlightenment. You can't journey toward a place when you are already there.

Instead, treat life as a moment-by-moment removal of the ego blocks that are put in front of your eyes, and which are preventing you from recognizing your fabulous, loving, 'divine' nature. Ego also stops you fully seeing the fabulous, loving, divine nature of others. You simply need to wake up to the realization. Almost like arriving in a new town and not knowing you have arrived, as you haven't been there before. Life is about removing the blocks that prevent us from seeing the true nature of who we are. The block is the ego and the many faces and aspects of the ego. The reason why the ego wishes to seek love and enlightenment, but not to find it, is that if the ego finds love, it cannot coexist with it. You can't have darkness where there is light; you can't have a lie where there is truth. If it is the ego's wish to destroy itself, it simply can't. It is only ever the ego that seeks self-improvement, as the love part of us does nothing but love *what is*. You can't fight fire with fire. So the only way to remove the blocks to finding your divine nature is to see every aspect of yourself as being divine already – and that includes your ego. If you love what you hate, how can you hate it? Fighting it just involves chasing your tail. Fully accepting your shadow makes it smaller; running away makes it bigger.

Love versus fear

Humans have an exceptional ability for consciousness and understanding. Yet we don't know how to live in balance in a dualistic world. As I touched on earlier, polarities are everywhere and all emotions can be placed somewhere on a spectrum that has **love** at one end and **fear** at the other.

You might think that the opposite of love is hate, yet love and hate are but horns on the same stag; they are born out of the same impulse. Hate is not the opposite of love. Hate is love corrupted by fear. Likewise, courage is not the opposite of fear, but rather it is love in spite of fear. In fact, love and fear are the only two emotions there are, as every other emotion is born of these two opposites. As I discussed earlier, thoughts and feelings at the love end of the spectrum are of a high, light, positive vibration, while those at the fear end are of a lower vibration and dull, heavy, and dense. Fear is mistrustful. Fear separates and isolates us. Love is joyful, hopeful, trusting, and optimistic. Love brings you closer to the full experience and expression of yourself. Love joins us together, allowing us to see that we are all intimately connected.

Don't get me wrong; the ego is also a fantastic self-understanding program. Learning what we are not takes us closer to understanding what we are. The ego is in place to protect our vulnerable physical body. The ego resonates with fear, so we don't go hugging bears, swimming with sharks, or allowing someone else to eat the last brownie. Sadly, the ego also protects us by chopping down trees, catching the last cod, and making sure its needs are met before those of the greater good. But we would still never eat the last brownie, at least, not when anyone is looking! This is the unbalanced ego that currently infects most of humanity.

Take a look at the following words to get an idea of the ego self as opposed to the more spiritual self.

Ego	Love
Fear	Love
Competition	Cooperation
Insecurity	Self-belief
Pessimism	Optimism
Control	Freedom
Greed	Balance
Boredom	Enthusiasm
Illusion	Truth
Despair	Hope
Cursing	Blessing

The lower chakra points resonate with the ego-based words. You could think about the bottom three chakras – root, sacral, and solar plexus – as connecting with the ego's need for physical connection through wants and needs. Through the solar plexus the intuitive ego frisks people to see if they are safe for us to be with. This might be felt as a sense of unease in the body or a *gut instinct* acting as a warning. If you are used to feeling a strong sense of somatic intuition, you might find it's not as trustworthy a tool as you thought. The gut deals with limitations and protection rather than expansion. The bottom three chakras also stay inside the body and don't come out the other side. Not all teachers who understand the chakras agree with this, but from my intuitive knowing, I don't feel that they come out of the back of a person.

From the heart chakra upward – heart, throat, third eye and crown – the chakras are connected more to the love and spirit part of who we are and give rise to mental, spiritual, and emotional intuition.

When the ego is in charge of the decisions you make in life, it can only decide in a limited way, as the decision will be made from the viewpoint of what is 'best.' The ego wants to make a decision to avoid as much pain and disappointment as possible. This view puts a limit on growth and the possibility of real, positive change. The kind of change that is sustainable for the greater good. The ego looks for a quick, pain-free fix. This is why the ego opens us up to addictions and limiting thoughts about ourselves. Stress and either too little or too much personal space can take us into ego thinking in a more attached way.

The ego faces

The ego is made up of many sub-personality voices, which we have constructed as emotional masks to protect us. Some of these masks were made in childhood as we learned those aspects of ourselves that were accepted and which were not. As the ego is all about self-protection, it looks for what will be agreeable to the 'tribe' and what won't be. It is not so worried about being authentic, but more about how to get its needs met. In this modern age, in a Western culture, as long as you can make money you can meet your needs. But the ego doesn't know that; it still believes that if you don't fit into the tribe, you'll be kicked out of the cave and starve. Hard to believe the ego hasn't noticed grocery stores! However it has noticed that grocery stores don't give food away for free. So the ego has moved into business.

Now the ego is the foundation of the career ladder, and develops sub-personalities for protection and progress. We then believe these sub-personalities and voices in our mind create who we are. We believe that we are only our personality. Yet our personality fluctuates and changes with every circumstance and situation life throws our way. We change because we bring forward a different mask to cope in that situation.

So who are we? We are a composite of the personalities we have created, based on what we have made the events in our past mean, and we are love. If our future is decided by the personalities we made in our past, we can only ever decide to recreate our past as we are making the same choices.

We find ourselves meeting the same types of people and finding the same life restrictions and limits. We find patterns that we can't seem to move on from. We may even see ourselves living the same life and being the same as our parents. We don't change our class structure or fall in love with someone who is outside our level of understanding. It would be a tall order to ask anyone to just forget everything they've learned about the world and have new ideas based on no evidence. The problem we have is that we have repeated evidence for what we know as we keep recreating it.

However, this situation isn't as impossible as it sounds. The smallest shift in ideas can move you off the track leading to the same limiting experience. In mathematics we understand that a small change alters everything. Life is chaos and yet has a divine, mathematical order to it. When you change one thing, you change the course of everything: A butterfly flaps its wings in the English countryside and sets off a hurricane in the Caribbean. It all starts with a decision in the mind. Changing how you think, from logic to intuition, changes the course of everything.

Knowing who is talking

The place to start is to know who is talking when it comes to your sub-personality mental voices. It is possibly less important to know where the sub-personality originated because we all have similar archetypes from different causes in our past. We often spend more time thinking about what caused a problem in our psyche than looking at how to move on from it. Looking at our issues only makes them bigger, if we give them too much energy. My reason for having a 'court jester' archetype might be completely different from someone else. Thinking that our sub-personalities are bad as such and knowing where they come from often creates judgment rather than gratitude. We also then spend too much time in a position of blame rather than taking responsibility for who we are.

In truth, knowing why we have created a mask through fear should allow us to have self-understanding, realization, and gratitude to ourselves for having found a method of survival. It might be redundant now, but at the time it was the best we could do. We were children learning and we still are, and so are our parents. Some archetypes still have a purpose in our lives and always will. For example, if I didn't have an inner 'pleaser' how would people like me? Would I become selfish?

Unfortunately in this dual-based universe, we often look for a negative realization about ourselves. Sadly, this is a way the ego uses self-development as a way to sabotage us from finding self-love.

One way to resolve this is to not fight it. One of the most spiritual realizations is to know that you and everyone else are, to a certain degree, imbalanced. No one is perfect. Forget it and forgive yourself and, if you can, others too. Love what you want to change, that way you allow it to move through you. Trying to change it without love simply makes it stick harder.

The sub-personalities

Here is a list of sub-personalities or archetypes; it is by no means complete because there are many more, but these are a few better-identified ones:

- Magician
- Child (orphan, wounded, frightened)
- Clown
- Controller
- Prince/princess
- Pleaser
- Father/mother
- Guru
- Healer (counselor)
- Hero/heroine
- Critic
- Martyr

- Mystic
- Prostitute
- Rescuer
- Saboteur
- Victim

You can, of course, see positive and negative sides to all these personalities as they coexist within you. Having a personal awareness, connection, empathic understanding, and form of communication with these sub-personalities gives us the opportunity to be able to talk them out of following the same patterns in life. It also means you can tell whether it is your ego talking or your intuition. You know which decisions are from the love part of yourself and which are from the ego. I can't say that the ego never makes a good move in your life, but it will be done with a much smaller stride than love makes.

If you want to identify your sub-personalities, you can do this by using your imagination. If you remember, the movie screen of the mind onto which the imagination plays is in the right hemisphere of the brain. The imagination is also our link to the subconscious mind. As the sub-personalities are the conscious mind's voice, it is really difficult to see them from the same place that they speak from. It's a bit like trying to listen to yourself singing, you always sing more quietly so you can hear yourself. In order to see them you have to allow the subconscious to speak in the right hemisphere of the mind. We can do this via the imagination. Using the imagination doesn't mean that whatever emerges from our imagining isn't real; it can be more real than reality.

Calming the ego mind

Many people believe that it is impossible to stop the thinking voice without meditation. In addition, many people believe they can't meditate because they are still thinking. If you are in the present moment and not thinking of the past or the future, you are in a form of meditation. Sitting in one position for a prolonged session of meditation can become uncomfortable and even painful. Being in awareness of physical pain is still part of meditation; wondering when you can get up and stretch your leg isn't. Your thinking voice is the same as your speaking voice, and so your inner and outer voice is the same. When I am talking I can't have a conscious thought at the same time: If I am in a library, or on a silent retreat, I can stop talking easily. We can stop thinking in exactly the same way. The reason we don't is because the ego mind makes us believe that we can't stop thinking. Even worse than this, it gives us feelings that if we do stop thinking, something bad will happen. It comes up with some crazy arguments against the idea of stopping thinking. For example, if you stop thinking, how would you know there was a bus coming as you cross the street? And would you forget your house keys? And so on.

The trick is to tell your mind that you have made a promise to be silent, and it just stops talking. Of course, it can start again if triggered by an external influence such as the phone ringing, but on the whole it stops and the observer takes over. The observer looks at the detail around us and makes no judgment. It merely observes beauty with curiosity; it enjoys the sense of life all around us, taking place within us, and being expressed through us.

Just walking the dog

I like to silence my thinking voice by walking my dog.
I go from thinking about what I need to do and telling
myself off for what I didn't do, to feeling the joy of
being in nature. Something as simple as crushing a dry,
fallen leaf underfoot brings such a sense of satisfaction
and joy. My mind observes the sensations, the feel of
the breeze, my dog's big doggy grin, or the sun and
the colors in nature. I am completely in the moment
and my senses are satisfied with all that there is in that
moment: I am perfect and all is well.

It is only the ego that exists in the past and the future.
It is all the ego thinks about. When it becomes silent,
the only place we can be is in the moment, where
we are intuitively listening with the right hemisphere
of the brain and receiving all there is to know in the
world. We become connected in unconditional love,
the universe and me. Then some total idiot comes
past too close on a skateboard and I want to kill him:
'I was connected to the divine cosmic unconditional
love right then you *idiot*!' Then being human with
an ego comes back like a bolt. The truth is the kid
on the skateboard is likely to be more connected in
meditation than I am. However, I'm sure if you're the
Dalai Lama, unconditional love is sustainable.

So be gentle with yourself. It is possible, with the ego under the control of your awareness, that you can be guided in the direction of your heart until, after a time, the ego comes back with the question: 'What shall I have for dinner?'

The monster sub-personalities

Depending on your life experience, some sub-personalities can feel stronger than the real you. Feelings of low self-esteem, lack of confidence, and even self-hatred can make you feel that there is no point trying to get anywhere in your life. This then becomes a fear of moving forward, which takes two parts: First, fear that you will let yourself and others down and won't be able to cope with what life brings; second, that everything goes well and that you are wrong about yourself. You don't know who you are without the story of your failings. Then life gets really scary, as you have to really live and have much more to lose. This can lead to the body even acting out the fear of moving into the future by running itself down with depression and fatigue. Of course, the body 'failing' in this way then becomes more evidence not to move forward.

What if fear/ego was a car? Fear can see through the darkness to the road ahead by using the headlamps. It has control over the brakes and, as long as it is driving in the same direction without changing course, it can tootle along. Of course, the roads of life are never straight; there are twists and turns, hills that go up and down, even mountains. However, it is okay because your inner knowing/intuition/observer is in the driving seat. It can see all the dials on the dashboard. It knows if you need more food, water, or rest. It can see the road signs directing you to interesting destinations, places of retreat, and where to refuel. It knows to change down a gear when the going gets tough for an uphill climb. It knows when to stop at the top and look at the view and what you have accomplished.

However, if there is a disconnect between the fear/ego in charge of the brakes and the inner knowing/intuition/ observer driving the car, fear can slam on the brakes and make the car stop still. Of course, if the car stays stopped then the car will start to decay. The brakes will jam, rust will start to form, and the car will fall into disrepair. Other transport that once traveled with you on the road of life will have no choice but to overtake and continue on without you. Of course the more attention you pay to the fear, the more time you're not in the driving seat.

Removing fear

It's ridiculously simple. The more attention we give to any aspect of ourselves that we view to be negative, the bigger we make that aspect. Sometimes therapy doesn't help as the focus is on the problem and even looking for the solution focuses on the problem. The more fuel we give fear, the bigger it gets. Luckily, the more fuel we give our intuition and knowing, the bigger it also gets. The problem here is that this approach relies on no evidence. There is often plenty of evidence in our life to believe that we are worthless. But going beyond the feelings of worthlessness takes faith.

Often people find this faith in something outside of themselves, such as religion or God. We all have an aspect of God inside us. We all have an inner creator that comes from our imagination. You may not have experienced an all-powerful incredible you, but you can imagine what it would be like to be that. From that point of imagination, manifestation begins. We start to find the evidence in small ways. Life rarely gives us anything we can't handle. So the movement toward positive thinking begins to turn around our life experience and the experience of ourselves. It is stunningly powerful. Of course, the ego will come up with some sabotage, such as saying, 'I don't have an imagination,' or 'I've tried everything and nothing works,' or 'the doctor says I have a syndrome,' or 'My childhood was so bad' – any number of reasons. The truth is that any emotion, including anger, above despair is an improvement.

There are lots of different self-help answers out there, but the only answer I have found that makes the focus on a problem transformational is to laugh. Laughing is the only thing that seems to cut through all emotions. When I've sat with clients while they have been feeling any of these emotions, they can still laugh.

Laugh in the face of your own weirdness and sense of lack of self-worth. Take away the importance of your situation. Of course it is important, but seeing it as important doesn't make it better. Loosening the grip of its importance also means that the importance loosens its grip on you. In that split second you might just get your foot on the gas long enough for the engine in your heart to roar into life again.

Using intuition for the removal of blocks

From time to time, we all get to a point in life where we feel blocked. This could be a creative block, such as writer's block where we just can't seem to make a start on the blank page. Often life offers us a blank page. We have to make a new career start, find a new relationship, or make friends in a new place. A block usually comes from blankness. The reason that a block is blank is because we are waiting for more information to fill the space. Our intuitive self can provide the information that the mind is banking on finding, thus turning a block into a holding point.

In fact, I would go as far as to say that there is no such thing as a block. Just a holding pattern while we are waiting for more information, like a plane waiting to land until it receives information from the control tower. Our intuition can be the control tower to let us know when to land or even when to take off. Mostly what creates the blank space is a sense of fear about the next step. This is a mini-version of being paralyzed with fear. It just blanks the creative mind out cold. The fear can take on many different guises and in a way it really doesn't matter what the cause is, as the root cause will always be to stop you finding love.

The truth is you have all of the answers you need for your life inside of you. That might sound clichéd but sometimes the reason it is hard to see them is because the answer isn't always easy. We don't always get to be in a situation where one path feels better than the other; sometimes both paths feel difficult. The ego only wants to find the easy path; however, sometimes that path is the longest in terms of pain – rather than a quick pull of the Band Aid and it's done. Your inner knowing will always go for the path that doesn't lead to a repeat of the situation. It always goes for the root of deepest learning. It makes more sense to go that way, rather than being in avoidance of discomfort, when you really know that is what you need.

Often a holding point will come because you don't want to look at the options for change. Change is scary. In fact, once you have mastered becoming comfortable with change, you have taken away one of the biggest causes of procrastination and repetition of problems. When you can trust your intuition then you can trust your decision-making progress. You may be surprised at how many people just can't make a decision because the mind is giving them too many options. The inner knowing only gives one option; the one you should take.

When you first get started with trusting your inner knowing, you might like to test what you intuitively know. One way to do this is to pose the situation or question as a curious feeling in your body. Then take a book or magazine, flip to a page at random and run your finger down the page until you want to stop. Often there, under your finger or in a nearby paragraph, is the answer to your question. Even if the answer isn't fully clear, you will find something that your intuition can use to search for deeper meaning.

Evolve and forgive

We all carry an energy system as I described earlier; however, included in part of that energy system is what Eckhart Tolle eloquently calls the 'pain-body,' and is best described in his book *A New Earth*.

My understanding of the pain-body is that it is an energetic membrane, which comes from energy created by our ego, when we feel any variations of hurt. As all thoughts create a vibration, they all create energy, too. This dense, dark energy sits around you until you deal with it. Often during our lives we have the opportunity to sort it out and heal; it draws toward it similar situations that caused the pain in the first place. We then find negative patterns forming, and the way to clear them is to behave differently in every repeated situation until you find the one that works. A bit like the movie *Groundhog Day* in which Bill Murray wakes up every day to the same challenges, over and over again.

In this way you can identify when the same patterns are coming up in your life. You find yourself with the feeling that this has happened before, but the absolute worst thing you can do is put this down to being 'your luck,' sit back, and look for evidence that the world is being unfair to you personally. You might think it is some kind of karma or because you're a nice person that other people abuse you repeatedly. But by choosing to buy into the idea that this is just 'my lot' in life, you deepen your pain-body and give a right to its existence in your life. It is difficult to be grateful for such a hard message, but it is only a message telling you about the need for change. The problem comes when we don't know how to change. In my experience, the easiest way to change is to adopt Bill Murray's approach and make a different decision every time – except, unlike his character, take a different action for the positive.

Also, I have found that the only way to dissolve an aspect of the pain-body, so it doesn't need to keep repeating the message, is forgiveness and love. How you create those emotions is up to you: You might want to see a therapist, counselor, or psychiatrist; you may have your own ways of healing; you could just decide to choose differently the next time the same issue comes up.

It isn't always possible to understand where the past event that created your pain-body originated, but I believe the pain-body can come with us from one lifetime to the next, along with any major, unresolved issues from that life.

Forgiving wrongs

One of my clients had a skin condition, which meant her skin would become swollen with small blisters appearing. Tuning in with my intuition, I found that in a previous lifetime her family had burned her to death for bringing shame on them. We discovered that the blisters came either when she felt she couldn't trust someone or in a difficult emotional situation. Her skin condition didn't flare up again once she had sent forgiveness to those who wronged her in the past life. I'm not saying that it is that easy with everything. We can't always simply wave a magic wand of forgiveness for pain caused in childhood or past lives; it is a journey to transform our pain into learning. If it can become positive, we can forgive, as we can't stay angry about something that has benefited us.

Unreasonable behavior is often the result of an active pain-body. If you discover that you have a strong pain-body, avoid alcohol. When we drink alcohol we remove aspects of our conscious mind, allowing the pain-body to emerge.

The pain-body differs in intensity for each person. The more forgiveness that you practice – along with empathy, intuition, and understanding – the less you will add to your pain-body, as it seeks to make itself stronger and bigger. No one else is responsible for adding to it. It is what you make a situation mean to you that will quantify whether you add to a pain-body in any given situation.

TUNING IN TO WHAT YOU KNOW

- Listen to your voices and start identifying your sub-personalities. Avoid thinking of them in terms of 'bad' or 'good.' Your ego created them to serve a purpose: To avoid pain, deal with certain situations, and protect you. However, by knowing your different sub-personalities and understanding their original purpose or intention, you will be able to quiet them and tune in to your love – your intuition.

- Your ego is the sum of all your fears and, unfortunately, giving your negative traits or issues attention just makes them bigger. Your aim should be to focus on what makes you happy and feel good. In this way, you release your fears' hold on you; laughter is the best possible way to stop them in their tracks.

- We all carry a pain-body in our energy system but if you avoid giving it focus, you also avoid creating an environment of reaction and blame. It might not be easy but figure out a way to work through your pain-body instead: Evolve and do something different each time to get out of negative patterns, find a way to forgive past hurts, and bring in more love when it gets tough. Pain leads to learning so be thankful for the knowledge your pain-body has given you and then just, where you can, let it go.

Chapter 4
FINDING OUR LIFE'S PURPOSE

Life needs purpose; our everyday needs to have a purpose. Without purpose, we are void of an important aspect of what it is to be human.

The basic truth of life is that we are on a planet, which is traveling around something that burns (the Sun) and we are held down by gravity, which science doesn't fully understand (and I am sure an elastic band is involved somewhere). In short, we have absolutely no idea what it is all about, so we give life a meaningful focus. In a sense, it doesn't matter what the meaning is because we need to have a reason to live. If we didn't, the enormity of the answerless questions would fry our ego mind. So much so that, for many people, life might become unbearable. Most of us need something to believe in, not always in a religious or spiritual sense, but to have a reason for living. Even those people who believe that nothing happens when you die and you simply turn to dust, are often focused on telling everyone else about it. And, in your experience, you may have known someone who quickly lost their purpose and gave up on life when they retired.

Something connects within us when we have purpose. Getting out of bed in the morning is a joy; a light shines in our eyes. Purpose doesn't have to be anything monumental; it simply means something to you. My mother grows trees in pots and when they are big enough, she plants them in the local wood; she doesn't do this for herself but for the next generation. They say the best time to plant a tree is 20 years ago, the second best time is right now. I know many people who volunteer to make the world a better place. For me, the purpose of life is to choose love over fear and to keep on choosing love over fear. As we have discussed, love over fear is choosing love over ego, God over the devil. If we do indeed live lifetime after lifetime, the only thing we need to aim for is to choose love. Yet each lifetime gives us layers of the ego to overcome. How we overcome those layers is up to us, but the simple rule of thumb is to choose love over fear. That is life's purpose in the big picture.

Living on purpose

In the smaller picture of what it means for your day-to-day life, it is finding a way of life that fits in with the reason you decided to be born. Imagine that before you were conceived, when you were in the spirit world, some winged nymph presented you with a form – the pre-birth questionnaire. It is just typical that life would start with a form! On it you answered what you wanted to get out of this lifetime. It could have been based on your past lives, the lessons of ego and karma, and so you were taught a lesson that you knew you needed to resolve. The meaning of 'karma' is often misunderstood, but the general consensus is that when you do something stupid then the universe thinks you're missing some education, and shows you better, by doing it right back to you.

You would have considered the best ways that you could be of service to the world. What you wanted to give in this lifetime. But then you came into the physical body, grew up and were taught how the world works. Now you know that you have to have a job, earn money, get a home, and raise a family. All of a sudden, your life's purpose becomes about survival. The ego makes sure that you are looking after number one because it looks like that is what everyone else is doing.

Yet when we are not living our purpose, the light isn't shining from our hearts and life feels meaningless. We don't quite know what is wrong, but we know that something doesn't feel right. It is at this point that we look for the purpose. Some people look for a life-changing experience; some people don't look until they retire from work, and some intuitive people simply know they were born for some 'other' purpose.

Often, when we feel we were born to do something special, we believe it is our ego telling us this, but in fact it is often our ego telling us 'it's all your ego,' when it is in fact our higher consciousness that knows what we wrote on our pre-birth questionnaire. Intuition isn't a skill simply for the physical world; it is a way for us to tap into what we know at all of the different levels of our expanded consciousness. By becoming even just a little bit curious about why you decided to be born, your purpose starts to be revealed. One example of this might be finding patterns, such as butterfly numbers (this is when every time you look at the clock you see numbers such as 11:11, 21:21, and 15:15), and this is often a symbol of transformation. The more curious you become about why they are happening the more they happen. All levels of our awareness can be accessed through the four intuitive types: Mental, somatic, emotional, or spiritual. Rather than looking for our purpose in the external world, 'what job, business, or way of life,' intuition let's us know that we already know.

What do you want?

We know that the ego wants to protect us and get us what we want. If you've ever done any acting, one of the first ways to develop a role is to find out what that character wants in every scene, and what is behind every speech and every line. This is also true in life; behind everything we do and every conversation we have there is a want. Finding what we want in our life is an important aspect of our development. Finding out *why* the ego wants something is often overlooked. The reason for most of our balanced (ego and love) wants usually comes from the pursuit of happiness or safety. Unbalanced wants often come from fear of losing what we have or not getting what we want. We may also fear letting down other people and not living up to expectations.

Finding out what blocks you from having what you want in life is best achieved by looking at *why* you want it. You might want to be a famous actor because you didn't feel noticed as a child. That want isn't likely to sustain you throughout your acting career. Many people also don't know what they want because they don't know what will make them happy. They may have found something that they thought would make them happy, and then it didn't, so what next? Most of the time it doesn't matter what you do in life as long as you know *why* you are doing it and your reasoning is from a balanced place: One of love and ego.

What motivates you?

Understanding your motivations means you can understand why you want something at a deeper level. We then get to know whether we want it because of fear; a motivation that is unlikely to serve us in the long term. However, trying to apply intuitive knowing to the things that you want, but don't serve your greater purpose, is difficult because the signal is weak. You simply can't hear what your intuition is telling you because your wants are based in ego and fear. You can try to intuitively know if something is the right decision, when your intuition knows that the *whole thing* isn't in your best interests or that you are being distracted from something much more meaningful.

If you can't get a clear intuitive knowing then it is time to take a look at the reason you are motivated in the particular direction you are leading yourself. It is possible to use your intuition to be able to hear your ego's driving force. The way to do this is to enter into an intuitive dialogue with the voice in your head. You can ask a question and feel from where in your body the answer is coming. Your head may tell you one thing in answer to the question and your intuition will answer with something deeper. Questioning yourself, as if you are another person, brings out answers from your inner knowing that you might not have been expecting.

Your best life

I have two questions you might like to answer. These questions are very useful in helping to find a motivation for living your best life.

What don't you like about the world/humans?

Often, whatever bugs you the most is what you were born to play a part in changing, for the better. What you don't like in others might be a route for change in yourself. It can even be your 'groundhog day.' Your personal challenges are the inoculations you need for your greater journey. It is as if the challenges we experience make us a better vehicle for our service in this lifetime. Understanding what we don't like about the world gives us clues about why we decided to be born. It is not that you have to solve this issue alone but this 'annoyance' is a work in progress, to either accept it or to do something to bring more love toward it.

Once you have identified what annoys you most about the world or humans in general, now take a look at how much it shows up in your life. You might also find that there is a whole bunch of things that irritate you, only to find on closer observation that these are all systems of a bigger issue. For example, if you're upset by greed, corruption, and selfishness you might see that these are symptoms of a person coming from a perception of separation and fear. You might then reflect and see how many times in your life you have felt like you are there for everyone else and no one is there for you. Often you'll find what we don't like about the world shows up in our life but wearing a different hat. It is what we were born to heal: Sometimes we heal it in ourselves by trying to heal it in the world; sometimes we heal it in the world by healing it in ourselves. But no pressure, you're not the only one born with the same task; it is our collective intention that makes an impact on the evolution of mankind.

What are you doing when you like yourself the most?

Now, I do like a nice slab of cheesecake but cheesecake doesn't make me like myself. I am not a big fan of going to the gym but the gym does make me like myself. I feel a sense of achievement; in fact I would go as far as to say that I like myself when I am suffering.

Think of as many things as you can that make you like yourself and list them. Be mindful of not writing down things that simply make you happy. Often what makes you happy becomes unfulfilling. What makes you like yourself will always sustain you. When you look in the mirror, you like what you see when you live a life that makes you feel good about being who you are.

Open to your purpose

These two questions and their answers are often enough to start opening to your life's purpose and what you were born to do. You might find you are already on the right path or that some of the choices you have made in your life start to make sense. It might be that you always find yourself in relationships and friendships where you are healing the other person. By doing this, you discover that you like yourself the most when you are helping people, but you would rather not have this in your personal life.

Imagine if life really did start with a form and you could go back and change which boxes you ticked. You can. Whatever you signed up for in the contract of your life's purpose, you can change.

Use intention to fix it

Using intention you can change whatever isn't working for you. In my life, I changed attracting friendships with people who didn't support me, simply by deciding that I only wanted to support people in my working life. That one change meant I not only got fantastically supportive friends, but also ones who were willing to support my work, too. Whatever patterns you are repeating because of your purpose, you can look at them intuitively and see if they serve you or not, and then adjust accordingly.

Supporting your purpose

A spiritual practice, as part of your daily or weekly routine, helps you keep in balance with your purpose. When we are at our best, we are at the center of who we are. When we are stressed or exhausted, we often find that our personality changes to a person unrecognizable to our normal selves. The same is also true when we are on a roll. When we are the best of ourselves, we can sometimes be unaware of other people's boundaries. We feel great; unfortunately the people around us don't feel quite so good in our company.

The best of who you are is found somewhere in the middle. The purpose of having a spiritual practice is to give you a regular opportunity to check in with yourself. Being spiritual is about ownership of who you are as a person. Going to see a therapist could be seen as part of a spiritual practice, as could taking time in your week to check in with your personal development. Being the best person you can be is spirituality. Making the world a better place by simply walking into a space with a smile is spirituality. Personal development is an important part of the growth of your community, your family, and every interaction you make.

Yet often people believe self-development is constantly to seek betterment or even perfection. As you can probably guess by now, the belief in perfection is an ego state that is out of balance with the truth of who we are. The truth is that there is nothing wrong with you at your basic level.

A good metaphor for this is to picture yourself as a very basic bicycle. You have two wheels, a frame, and handlebars; everything you need for the road of life. Your basic bike is perfect. It needs nothing more to enable it to do its job of moving forward. But then something happens, someone tells you that life is difficult and you'll encounter many hills. So you get some gears. You then start to load the bike down with supplies on the handlebars; you might also want the bike to look better, so you paint it. You then might see someone else on a bike going faster than you and, even though they have more physical capacity, you half kill yourself trying to keep up. The truth is that your bike, without all the extra stuff, is perfect. Spirituality is about removing all of the bells and whistles from your basic bike to remind yourself that everything you are is enough. However, that can be a terrifying thought. What have you been working for all these years if you are already 'it'?

When you look at humanity's basic drive to move forward, to achieve success, or even reach enlightenment, it usually comes from a belief that we will then feel whatever we want to feel. This might be happy, relaxed, accomplished, full, worry-free, or any number or all of the positive feelings. When we let go of that belief, the motivation behind moving your bike forward becomes about the simplest things: To feel the wind in your hair, the sun on your face, to be witness to the beauty in the world, to find fellow riders to make the journey more of a joy in the times when the hills are steep, and simply to feel connected to something outside of yourself. These are the people who walk into a room with a sense of peace. You can still have goals, but the goals become less personal and more embracing of the things that truly matter, finding things to share rather than things to take. Knowing your purpose and having a spiritual side to you gives you balance.

You might like to say that spirituality is like having stabilizers on the bike; it means you won't fall over if pushed sideways by life. Having a way to check in with yourself brings you back to the basic bike. The idea is to stay in balance in the middle, knowing that there is nothing wrong with who you are but being mindful of what your ego is presenting to you, and how you in turn present that to the world. In a sense, the best way to be in the service of others is to be of service to yourself. When you have your center of balance, you bring less toxicity into the world with your fear triggers.

Holding a space

Whenever you are in an unbalanced situation, your balance becomes the tuning fork for the sound around you. So if you are in a situation of conflict at work you tune yourself back to love. It is the same answer as when you are with a friend who is having a hard time, you tune them back toward love. You don't have to give a sermon; you are that step closer to love. It also means that if a person is bending you out of your balance with their actions, you have a central place for your boundaries. Having a midpoint for your boundaries means that you know how far you are extending them. You don't give mixed messages by having an ever-changing level of self-esteem.

Avoiding ego spin

I was involved in a car accident once. It was a clear case of the other driver's error. However, I have been told many times never to apologize at the scene of an accident, as it is seen that you are taking the blame. The driver getting out of his car was clearly about to blame me. I smiled and said 'That was unfortunate.' After a few sentences, where he tried to blame me, he then went on to blame some construction workers a mile down the road for causing the traffic buildup. In fact, he blamed the accident on all sorts of things including the weather. The one thing he didn't see as being at fault was himself. Simply holding the space for him to have an ego spin was all I could do. When he finally stopped spinning, he was able to deal with what we needed to do to be on our way. Of course, his ego spin could have sparked a spin of my own.

Having a spiritual grounding means that no matter how triggered someone tries to make me, I will slow down their spin just by holding the space. It does make life easier. This was my spiritual service to the driver and also to myself.

. . . .

The ego wants to make other people 'wrong' and it justifies that it is right in doing so, by saying 'they are in the wrong.' But this is what people mean when they say 'two wrongs don't make a right.' They should also say that balance *can* make it right. This kind of centering isn't easy or possible without self-esteem.

Having a sense of purpose, a spiritual code, or a spiritual practice such as meditation goes a long way toward having a sense of self-esteem. When you know that you are a good person, you live more in balance and allow others to treat you better. Having a self-development practice and allowing this to show up in your interactions in your life is spirituality. Here are some ideas you might like to adopt:

- Meditation
- Yoga
- Swimming
- Seeing a therapist
- A weekly exchange with a friend
- Sitting in silence
- Walking in nature
- Being mindful
- Being in the moment
- Running

There are many ways to check in with yourself and keep your balance. Find one that works for you.

Know your values

Another way to stay in balance is to know your values. Your values create a safe container for all the decisions you make in life. If a decision resonates with your values, it can become part of your life; if it doesn't, it goes on the outside of your safe container. Knowing your values becomes a spiritual and moral code; it means that you can't be tempted into making choices that you may later regret. People who have values are often respected and trusted.

Trust is fundamental in any relationship. It is not up to someone else to trust you blindly; it is up to you to be constant in who you are in order to earn that trust. Trust is rooted in faith, and to have trust is to have a belief in someone. Trust is not to be taken lightly because when you break someone's trust, you break his or her faith. How many of us have had our faith in people broken over and over again? Yet we still have to live and to love. You have to have trust, you have to believe in someone, and then you have to have faith. Intuition can guide you to the people that you can trust. However, you have to be able to trust yourself first. This is the core of self-belief, which, unlike confidence, can never waver. The foundation stone of self-belief is sticking by your values.

Having values also means you recognize the people that you want to be in your life, resulting in a happier time and getting hurt less. As humans, we judge people. When you judge someone with love-based intuition, you will see both sides of who they are. When you judge someone with fear, you will only see the side that could harm you. Both ways of judgment are useful for self-protection but, interestingly, we often ignore what we know. The inner critic will tell us off for being judgmental. When you have values, if another person doesn't hold the same values as you it is unlikely that you'll be a match as friends, business partners, or lovers. You can still admire those people and be attracted to them; however, for safety they need to stay on the outside of the container.

Seeing the good

One of my patterns is seeing the good in other people and thinking that I can help them by loving them into change. Often I can see that their wall of self-protection, which causes them to lie or cheat, is due to bad experiences in their past. My belief is that I can show them a new world. Unfortunately, they tend to show me their world. It can take you longer to find lost faith than it can to find a new friend or partner. Your faith is valuable and too precious to lose. Help people, but only on the outside of your safe container. For me, that means as clients and not as friends.

Values are something we need to teach our children, as they are bombarded with media images teaching them the value of *stuff*. The value of money becomes greater than the value of life. This makes for an upside-down world. In recent years we have seen the outcome of a lack of values being expressed in business and politics. It is my belief that there will be a positive backlash, retuning to basic human values. We simply cannot have an ordered society without trust, as when we lose faith in other humans we have lost everything. Roger Steare, who describes himself as a Corporate Philosopher and Professor of Organizational Ethics, says:

> *'Journalists routinely ask politicians "tell us what your policies are." Why don't they start asking about their principles – their moral principles – as those are the foundations of a moral community?'*

Creating your safe container

Values are very simple. When you look through the list below, think about:

- What values you have that have meaning to you.

- What values you need to develop.

- What you value in other people.

- What values you would like to be associated with in your life and work.

You might like to make a list of these top values; don't expect them all to apply to you. In fact, a few core values might be of more benefit than a long list that is unsustainable.

- Solitude – time alone
- Time with friends
- Security
- Making a difference
- Freedom

- Cheerfulness
- Self-expression
- Patience
- Tolerance
- Comfort
- Honesty
- Adventure
- Being needed
- Independence
- Animals/pets
- Trust
- Love
- Creativity
- Peace of mind
- Environment
- Simplicity
- Integrity
- Education
- Intelligence
- Family
- Career
- Achievement
- Spirituality
- Political awareness

Not sharing *all* of the same values is perfectly acceptable, but some values will be fundamental. My value in honesty is a deal-breaker in any of my friendships or relationships. Because of this I have fewer friends, but what is a friend if it's not someone I can have faith in? Not to mention the fact that it's annoying as an intuitive to know that someone is lying to you, but out of politeness you can't say it. Calling someone a liar is a bigger taboo then being one.

Inner knowing

So how do you handle situations when you intuitively know that someone is telling you a lie? There is no way you can prove it in an evidential way. For example, I had to put my dog on a flight from San Francisco to New York. I did extensive research into the best airline – one where I could drop off and pick up my dog from inside the airport, and not two miles away in a cargo bay. This part of the journey is the most stressful for the dog. I found an airline that would do it in the best way possible. I asked lots of questions, checked, and double-checked the arrangements. Something felt wrong; I checked in with myself and really felt that this wasn't my paranoia coming through as ego fear and not intuition. I checked and checked again until I became annoying to myself, as well as the person on the end of the phone.

On the day of the fight, I checked in the morning with a phone call. The original arrangements were confirmed. Then I got a phone call to tell me that the office was closed at weekends and my dog would have to board the flight from cargo, exactly what I was trying to avoid by paying more money and going with this airline. My inner knowing was watching a slow car crash with no way to know exactly what was going to go wrong, and not able to stop it. Living through intuition, this will happen from time to time. There will be situations you are awake to, but can do nothing to stop happening. What creates an act of consciousness is how you handle it. Being enlightened doesn't mean you don't feel all of the uncomfortable emotions, it just means they move through you quicker.

. . . .

The wisdom of the Enneagram

What we think about life's purpose, we often think about in terms of a career or a way of living. We would like to have a purpose that is unique to us. In fact, humanity shares one purpose: To seek out love and overcome fear.

Our life's purpose is to remove all the blocks we have in place that stop us finding a profound sense of love. Every lifetime when we reincarnate, it is for the same purpose, although we might all be on different rungs of the ladder in terms of our closeness to love from one lifetime to the next. We see this in people's different values and personality types. I like the personality profiling known as the 'Enneagram.'

The Enneagram model defines nine personality types (which also define their worldview and motivations), which are illustrated by the points of a geometric figure called an enneagram from the Greek words *ennea* meaning 'nine' and *gramma* meaning 'written down' or 'illustrated.' The geometric figure also indicates the connections between the types, often a subject taught in academic psychology.

You could see these personality types as also linked to the evolution of the removal of ego blocks. As we move closer to love, we also see changes in our personality type. However, this isn't a numeric calculation, of which one is the best or worst personality; it just shows the blocks we are presented with in this lifetime.

Below are the nine personality types; don't expect to know yours simply from the description below – that might need some deeper inquiry.

1. Reformer: I must do everything exactly the right way.

2. Helper: I must serve others.

3. Motivator: I need to succeed.

4. Individualist: I am unique and romantic.

5. Thinker: I need to understand the whole world.

6. Skeptic: I am affectionate yet skeptical.

7. Enthusiast: I am happy and open to new things.

8. Leader: I must be strong.

9. Peacemaker: I am at peace.

People are complex, of course, and don't fit neatly into nine personality types. However, the sound/vibe/energy of a person can be broken down into frequencies of evolution. As an intuitive, you can start to recognize what sound a person is making, how it relates to sounds of people that you have known before, and how to group people according to their compatibility with yourself or others. You can also understand more about their needs and how they complement or contradict you. For example, a personality type seven, 'Enthusiast,' will not understand personality type four, 'Individualist.' The Individualist needs to really connect with their feelings about a situation before they can move on from it. The Enthusiast has already moved on and is having a brilliant time.

The wisdom of the Enneagram gives us ways of perceiving new pathways in our relationships and new ways of satisfying our deepest desire to get along and to be decent people. It also allows us to understand that people simply are at different levels of evolution. Frank De Luca, who teaches the Enneagram in San Francisco, says:

> *'You learn a lot of compassion and patience because you have a broader understanding of human nature. You see they're doing the best they can, based on the experiences they had in early life. Your strengths, when overdone, become your weaknesses.'*

Soul purpose

Looking at our personality is one way to look at how we evolve closer to love from one lifetime to the next, but there is also a shift in our very soul. There are lots of different schools of thought on the soul. Some think it is the feminine of the spirit; others that the soul is a different word for the 'spirit.' The way I am using the word, I mean the 'immortal energy' or 'consciousness,' which I believe lives on after the death of our physical self. The soul is not a 'thing' as the ego likes to think in terms of the physical world; the soul is a state of being.

The soul's path to finding its purpose is to be in connection with spirit, divine nature, the source, or God. This is a simplistic idea, but for simplicity's sake I believe souls can be split up into soul groups. Some people in the same soul group may be born within each other's lifetime to actualize each other's growth. This might be one way of explaining when a parent loses a child or when an amazing relationship ends in disappointment. You may need to reconnect to a beautiful connection, which may or may not be as fulfilling in a physical sense, but is perfect in your non-physical evolution. You might meet a 'soul mate' from a past life, but it doesn't mean the connection is definitely going to work out in this lifetime. Sometimes we simply reconnect in order to open up possibilities and nothing is preordained. These soul groups can be people of all different vibrations; they can be a complete mismatch as well as a match.

Souls can be split into seven frequencies of vibration. The ego would like to put them into a higher to lower sound vibration, from enlightened to dumb. Try and avoid that way of thinking if you can and instead think in terms of a circle. All of the frequencies are already who you are. If you think of yourself as a hot air balloon, how high you go depends on how light you are, so the more baggage you've dropped, the better. We are all balloons; just because one balloon can't go as high as another balloon due to holding onto baggage doesn't stop that balloon from having the potential to fly. It is a case of letting go of fear and allowing yourself to fly.

Level one souls like a simple life. They may stay in one job or live in one place. They don't leave what they have for fear of losing it.

Level two souls can see that there is more to life and then start to question and look for answers. They often find religion and will stick to it wholeheartedly, sometimes becoming fanatical.

Level three souls start to wander and will travel and play many roles in life.

Level four souls feel the need to create for others, but often for money or notoriety.

Level five souls feel the world is a terrible place; they feel a sense of disconnection from everyone and everything, sometimes ending their life prematurely as nothing seems to work for them.

Level six souls just want to give to others and will sometimes have trouble with boundaries, but feel a need to spread love.

Level seven souls are immersed in awareness and being.

The souls beyond these numbers are probably not coming back to tell us about it, although I've met a few. My ego is absolutely convinced that I am somewhere at the top! But I laugh it off. And on that note, it is always worth remembering we are the balloons not the fear (ego) that keeps us grounded.

Moving up

Our life's purpose is about moving up through these frequencies. Removing the blocks we have that prevent us from seeing others and ourselves as loving beings. If you want to keep moving up the ladder, find out your values and stick to them. They become a compass by which you base your truth. Keeping honest to you, not justifying bad actions or making up stories, is the best way to head up the ladder. The voice in your head is a fabulous storyteller, but it's only our intuition that can tell us if the story is true. Stay curious and questioning of everything that gives you less then lovely emotions. The chances are you have told yourself something somewhere in your past that wasn't true.

For me, when I step out of my thoughts I find them very funny; and what I find hilarious is when I think they are oh, so very important and then I really laugh. I laugh like a mad woman who has found sanity.

Assisting others

Understanding someone else's path also means that you are less likely to try and fix other people. You can assist other people on their journey, by being the most loving and authentic person you can be. You can do this by not buying into their story but not discrediting their right to believe it either. Doing more than that means we start to interfere with another person's freewill, even when we love that person and only want the best for them. Giving someone else your awakened vision, when they haven't asked for it, is never wise.

Tuning out

A while ago I developed gallstones due to hereditary coeliac disease. Two days before my first ever surgery to have my gallbladder removed, I was confronted by someone telling me that 'spirit' was telling them I must not have the operation. That it was my karma, I had something to learn, the surgeon was going to 'butcher' me and 'I could remove the stones later with a liver flush.' I didn't mind the opinion, but the problem was someone giving an opinion power by underlining it with 'We were meant to meet,' 'I have been sent to tell you,' or 'It's no coincidence that my bulls**t has found you today.'

. . . .

The truth is if you want to be a savior, you need to find someone who needs saving. It is often the vulnerable who needs saving. It is the ego that feels great when someone takes our advice. Luckily I didn't listen to this guy, as my intuition is so strong, I knew there was no getting out of this surgery. It was lucky as it turned out to be a bit more complex on the inside of my body, and if I had followed his weighted opinion I would now be dead. No matter whether you're intuitive, psychic, a medium, connected to the angels, or dancing with fairies, if you're alive you have an ego. Even a great mystic has to be skeptical of the voices in their head.

The need to help other people comes from the ego. The need to love other people comes from your loving self. Perhaps by asking me to talk about the surgery, giving an opinion in this way 'have you thought that maybe you can xyz?' I would have felt heard and loved. It would have given loving power to me, not disempowered me. However... I still might have wanted to hang him by the socks!

While we're on the subject, there can be a lot of judgment around ill health, that you somehow manifested it purely from being a negative person. More often than not we learn so much from difficult times, you have to ask yourself, did I manifest a great lesson here? Or did I manifest ill health? It's often hard to separate the two.

Avoid the drama

People will often try and pull you into their life dramas, to authenticate why it is impossible for them to find love. If, because you love them, you get pulled into their drama, too, then you are siding with the ego. At some point you will have to pull out and, in doing so, prove the ego right.

The stories we tell ourselves are so important; the words we use and our perception of those words embellish a dramatic tale. My dog stepped out in front of a slow-moving car, I caught her in time and, although she was shaken, she wasn't hurt. I however went into the drama of 'she was almost hit by a car!' and had the same amount of stress as if a car traveling at 30mph had nearly killed her. She was fine, and I realized I was reacting to 'perceived drama' and not the real situation. The dog had no idea of what happens when a car hits you so she was over it really quickly. Your take, or even spin, on a story makes the difference between being empowered or disempowered by it.

Hero, victim, or survivor

I was 17 when a boy I really liked kissed me under the boardwalk of the seaside town where I spent my teenage years. When he tried taking it further he wouldn't take 'no' for an answer. This could have been the drama where a man tried to rape me, but instead it is the event where I learned the power of fingernails in eyeballs. A few years later, while backpacking in Australia, a man who had escaped a mental institute grabbed me from behind. Afterwards, when the police interviewed me, they cautioned me that running after the man and continuing to attack him could be considered assault and to let the matter go. Would that situation have turned out differently, if I had a different belief about myself? I think so.

. . . .

You decide your character in the stories of your life. You decide if you are the hero, victim, or survivor. You can even name the chapters in your life differently:

Chapter 1: I Was Born or The Coming of the Chosen One

Chapter 2: My Parents' Divorce or The End of the War

Chapter 3: I Nearly Died or I Survived

This is why it is so important not to buy into other people's stories or project your negative story onto other people's lives. It weakens them. So when someone tells you their plans don't give them horror stories of how it could all go wrong and don't buy into the tales of horror that you hear.

Choose your role

My mother was involved in an accident, and afterwards she sat on the settee looking broken. My heart bled for her, and I just wanted to make her feel better. She said 'This is the worst thing that has ever happened to me, and I don't think I'll ever fully recover.' 'WHAT? I'm not buying into that,' so I pointed out all the things that she had survived, all the amazing things she had done. Her body changed, she sat up a little more and said 'You're right… I'm not this victim woman. I'm that survivor woman.'

. . . .

When a client comes to see me it is often about having limited perception. This is the definition of a block; a block is a holding point while we are stuck with a limited perception of a situation, the world, or ourselves. Blocks in our present perception are often due to what we made our past mean – not what actually happened. So you can see why it is important to know whether you are, for example, a survivor or a victim. Using intuition I look backward to see where the limiting belief started, we then unravel the limiting belief, thus getting life back into flow. The ego needs stories and characters (archetypes), but the truth is if you play a limiting role you will never get a leading part in your life. Someone else will play a tune and you will dance to it.

By becoming intuitively curious about ourselves, we have the chance to understand the story we are being told by other people, and the stories we are telling ourselves. You can feel intuitively when a story isn't true by analyzing how it has been embellished to give it drama, and then just step out of it.

TUNING IN TO WHAT YOU KNOW

- Open to your true-life purpose by understanding what gives you self-esteem and makes you feel good about yourself. Once you understand what you are 'here' for and are operating from a 'safe container' of values then you will find it easier to distinguish between the right and wrong decisions and the right and wrong people for you.

- The more you carry on loving and don't authenticate the drama of someone else's life experience (or your own), the happier you will be, and the more you will be able to bring others out of their rotational drama. By being still and connected to love you can inspire people to do the same; they hear the sound you are sending and tune in to you. Conversation just creates arguments, but silent love defuses drama.

- All of us have created blocks that stop us from being able to realize that we are already enlightened loving beings. Even seeking ways to remove the blocks is a distraction from the truth that we are love. Having a block means your perception is restricted and puts you into a holding pattern while you wait for more information. The only information you really need to remember is that we are beings of love; we just put blocks in the way of seeing that. To open up the view the best thing we can do is attack life with a large dose of humor. I have often found that the love flows in the gaps between the laughter.

Chapter 5
WHAT I SEE IN YOU,
I *KNOW* IN ME

The more you see your ego, the more you can trust your intuition and also spot when other people are coming from their ego. You might even be able to spot the various sub-personalities and aspects of the pain-body. The dilemma you now face is 'Should I tell them?' How would you tell them? And is it even important to tell them? Unfortunately no one likes feeling as if they are being criticized, analyzed, or judged. So, no matter how excited you are about sharing your insight, you must do so with care. There is an Aboriginal saying 'You cannot teach what the student isn't ready to learn,' yet everyone likes to be heard and feel fully understood.

The more you listen to another person, the closer a relationship you can have. What also allows intimacy and avoids hurtful disagreements is to be mindful of what triggers our ego from our past. The ego loves to be right and make others wrong, simply because it then feels it will get a bigger piece of the carcass as the alpha in the tribal pack. It is also safest to be the smartest person in the room (though often the loneliest). With your newfound power, through information, comes great responsibility; you now have to ensure that your communication stays authentic as much as possible. You know conversation can involve small talk, banter, and gossip. Life would be dull if we didn't have the odd conversational sparring match, but when it comes to loving communication, we must seek out the truth and communicate from that place. The truth is never going to be from our ego. The ego is just going to be about stuff that we think things mean, rather than what they truly mean at a deep level.

Intuitive listening

I was asked if there is any way that you can intuitively know if your partner will cheat on you. While this is a meaningful question, it is not as interesting as the fear behind the question. You might think it's a simple fear – 'I will be betrayed and it will mean the end of our relationship.' The question might be coming from the belief 'I am not good enough for my partner, so will I be able to continue to convince them that I am good enough?' If we continue to deal with the symptoms of fear and ego in conversation, we never really make a true connection that can bring about valuable change in a person's viewpoint. The first question I ask a client is 'What do you want to get out of this session?' I then don't think about how to answer what they say, I wonder what's beyond the question. The deepest insight is to be found right there.

Let's put you in that situation. Your partner asks, 'Have you ever cheated on me?' The ego's reaction is likely to be one of hurt – 'You don't trust me?'

The first level of listening to someone is always accompanied by the ego whispering, 'What about me!' The second level of listening is to deal with the symptom. 'Why do you think I would cheat on you? I would never do that.' The third level, intuitive listening, is an awareness of everything that is being said and what is unsaid: the spaces in between the words, the body movements, emotion, energy, vibration, and the full expansion of knowing. You might even decide not to reply. You might then hold that person and let what needs to emerge come through. It might be something as simple as having put on some body weight, which is making the person feel insecure, and nothing about you or the relationship at all.

At this point, blurting out that it is only your inner critic sub-personality might not be the most useful thing to do. But because you 'know' where the fear is coming from, it means you can bring it to an authentic place and not have a bad situation in your relationship. Just because someone is dreaming in the ego state, it doesn't mean that the dream doesn't feel real and very nasty.

 Being heard

When I was living in New York, I met a man in Washington Square Park as I was walking my dog. It was 7:15 a.m., and the start of another sweltering hot day. This man had just woken up having slept the night on the grass. As he walked up behind me, my dog became fearful and agitated as the man clearly had mental health problems; he was shouting and cursing. Sometimes, long-term use of drugs or alcohol, or a life that has involved trauma, will mean a person will get stuck into a paranoid victim sub-personality. This man was showing all of those symptoms, yelling about being wronged in such a fast-talking way you couldn't fully make out what he was saying, except for the odd 'F' bomb, 'N' bomb and 'B' bomb (sorry this book doesn't come with a list of the meanings of these profanities at the back, now please stop thinking about what a 'B' bomb is and read on.)

As he came close, I pulled to one side as my dog was really freaking out; that's what dogs do when they are on a lead and danger approaches. The simple move of pulling to one side looked like an act of fear on my part. The man came and stood in front of me, way too close for comfort. In that moment, mine was the face of everything he felt wronged by in his life. As he was yelling at me, I held my ground and kept his eye contact. I listened to everything he had to say as intently as I could, keeping my breathing steady even though I could feel energy running all over my skin telling me to run. As I kept listening, his power started to drain and he started to become curious about me. He stopped and asked, 'Have you got nothing to say for yourself.' I slowly shook my head with apology in my eyes, even though it wasn't me and my generation that brought slaves into the USA, even though he was never a slave, in my DNA was an apology to his DNA and although I didn't understand him, I did understand his pain. It is only the pain I can address, not the rights and wrongs, truth or untruth, just the pain. 'Nothing to say? I didn't think so,' he said and stormed off shouting and with the odd backward glance toward me.

· ·

My point in telling this story is that everyone wants to be heard, even a person who is misdirected. By simply taking a moment to listen, we heal. Now, the dog and I didn't deserve to have a man yelling at us before coffee. I'm sure he didn't deserve to have a life that led him to sleeping in the park. We deal with what we have, and what we all have is the gift to intuitively pay attention. I am lucky; I knew that I wasn't going to be hurt by him. I also knew if I told him where to go, I would have got hurt. That's the gift of inner knowing. It means that it is possible to react in love and not in fear. Every moment is a chance to give a gift; mostly it is a gift to you.

Intuitive connections

The expansion of this level of listening with your inner knowing is wonderful for all aspects of life and, in particular, with your family. Understanding your parents to this level means that we don't keep putting them in a box of 'good' or 'bad.' We put them in the box marked 'human.'

Listening with inner knowing

One of my students asked me how to intuitively understand her mother, as she sets out with great intentions and yet every phone call ends up with her losing her temper. We build layers and layers of pain.

Her (and your) mother is in reaction to her mother in reaction to her mother and so on. Knowing intuitively why someone acts the way they do significantly helps, but it doesn't change them, it changes you. It enables you to know what triggers you, and to understand why parents act the way they do. Our actions toward another's ego can allow someone to step into the space outside their ego and often they do change.

However, we can't act to make that happen, as then it is still coming from the ego. We simply pick up the phone to make a call with the intention of healing, nothing else. We enter a room to heal the room, and somehow we heal ourselves and the other people within the room, too. It means that we can tap into a level of forgiveness without the 'guilty' party needing to seek atonement. Often it is difficult to forgive, when we feel someone didn't understand the true implications of what they did. Yet if we can understand the level of their misjudgment or folly, we can forgive without them needing to even understand what they did.

· ·

Intuitive listening is also powerful in the workplace. The workplace is riddled with ego as we are triggered into primitive responses: 'I lose my job and I am out of the social cave, and I will starve.' The ego doesn't know or trust that you will get another job. Or that it could be the biggest blessing, as you take a more empowered path. So the need for ego safety causes us to want *power over* rather than giving *power to*. In my life, when I've been employed I have inspired people (mostly women) to bully me. This pattern went on for many years, in many jobs, with different perpetrators, until one day I walked into the office and caught my boss off-guard. She didn't see me, but in her body and her energy I felt her vulnerability. It made me soften, so when she looked up she could finally see me. She could see my energy wasn't defensive – it was open. I asked her how she was feeling, and I meant it. From that moment, she never bullied me again.

Relationships, family and work are where this kind of intuitive connection with people works best. If you extend this 'connection' into the wider community then you expand the possibilities of bringing positive change.

Community and a sense of belonging

I love community because it is so amusing to see how much we try and avoid it, while saying we want it. You often don't meet the person living next door until the power is cut off and they, or you, need a candle. Whole streets of people get together when the local government has done something to take down the quality of the neighborhood. In apartment blocks, is there any need for everyone to own a vacuum cleaner? We don't share in case someone breaks it or doesn't clean it, or we get ripped off somehow. What about WiFi? Is there any need, where a house is split into two, for both parties not to share the WiFi and its cost? I think we would rather fry our brains on the electromagnetic field than share.

This mindset is now at the cost of our planet. The average Western person uses two to three times their share of the Earth's resources in one lifetime. Why don't we come together as a community? It's very simple… because the ego is scared of other human beings.

It wasn't always this way. The infrastructure of older countries such as the UK is set up for community living. During World War II food was rationed and people came together to swap food and other necessities. People in the country looked after strangers' children, who had been evacuated from the cities for safety. It had town centers, often with a clock tower in the middle and some kind of town hall. Sadly, the face of the UK's towns is starting to look bland and uniform, as chain stores take over the high streets with their brand image making each place a twin of the last town you visited. The community corner store, where you could get some good advice with your groceries, has almost gone. Those small businesses hanging on to their trade are often finding it hard to pay rent. Landlords are also being put under pressure to take contracts from larger chains, as they know they will get the rental income needed.

The USA is set up so that people drive their cars everywhere. Soulless shopping malls overwhelm you as you find yourself walking about in a trance, overpowered by all the advertising. Towns often don't have a center and the shopping mall is the place where young people meet. The coffee shop Starbucks saw this situation and created a meeting place where people could join together. The coffee shop industry has grown so much since the opening of the first Starbucks in Seattle. In 1990, there were 500 cafés in the USA, now there are 22,000 outlets worldwide and the chain continues to expand. Of course it is partly due to our coffee addiction, but also because it gives people a place to meet and be with one another.

From the isolation of people working from home, driving solo in their cars, and then meeting people over the internet, we are now seeing a backlash of people wanting to come together and unite. This is partly because of some of the wider issues we now face and partly because it is very lonely out there. Places like San Francisco are building community groups to grow their own produce on rooftops and getting homeless people together to grow food. The people of San Francisco have rejected the larger chain stores and have put pressure on the city government so that almost all waste is diverted from landfill and sent for recycling.

When communities get together to make change, it is powerful. Sadly, the reason we are not powerful and together is because we fear each other: not wanting to get caught talking to the old lady on the bus is a prime example. We fear a ten-hour in-flight conversation that we can't get out of with the person next to us, so we don't talk at all until close to the end of the flight.

Intuitively connecting means that you are empowered about *who* you talk to and how you hear them. Small talk with intuition can become the most interesting exchange. We only fear the ego in others, but you have the tools to bring someone from ego to authentic conversation, which can lead to fantastic opportunities.

Ego as a mirror

The ego aspects we see in other people are often highlighted, as they are aspects of our own self that we have to deal with or, more usually, try to deny. For example, when people put their feet up on the seats of public transport, I feel this annoyance that comes into my body. My mind then comes up with a story about that annoyance: 'That person is disrespectful, they don't care about other people, they are selfish, they wouldn't do that at home, and that's the kind of person who doesn't recycle.'

Of course, these are all stories; I don't know any of this to be true, given the evidence. Where the anger is coming from in me is to be questioned. First, I would love to put my feet on the seats. There is a rebel inside of me that wants to say 'screw the world.' I am annoyed that they allow themselves the freedom to do that. I have another coexisting story, 'I do so much for people and the planet, alone; am I the only one who cares?' The person with their feet on the seats is an indicator of my feelings of disconnect. I am also annoyed at my inability to ask them to remove their feet from the seat. So what is really annoying me? The one person with their feet up is triggering a whole story that I am making up in my head. I am not reading a wonderful book or looking at the view out of the window, and I am in danger of getting in a bad mood. Why? Because it justifies that I am a good person in the polar opposite of this situation. I am a good person; this is not a good person. Then I can justify past or future lapses in being a good person.

The dark side

A young man had a seat on the train while two older ladies stood. They loudly made comments about how men are no longer what they were and how disgusting it is not to be given a seat. He asked them, 'Who should have priority to sit down?' He knew the conversation was directed at him. They gave him a list: 'Old people, pregnant women, people with small children, the disabled, and women.' He then showed them his leg, which was notably shorter than the other and compensated for with a rather large, heavy boot, which he dropped like a hammer in front of them. Of course, it silenced the argument.

. . . .

The shadow

We all have a dark side, defined as the 'shadow' by Carl Jung, the psychologist who coined the phrase. It is a bit like the dark side of the moon – you just can't see it. The only way we see that side of ourselves is when it is reflected back to us in everything that we don't like about other people. It is as if they hold up a mirror to what we try to hide. You can also see it in the aspects of your personality that you pride yourself in. As everything works in polarities, whatever you like about yourself, you will find that the opposite of that quality is what you don't like in others or yourself. It is hard to work out what the opposite personality trait is exactly, but you might find something close.

For example, a person who is helpful might also be controlling; a person who is generous with money might be tight with time. The shadow is the part of ourselves that we disown. By knowing it is there and taking some ownership of it, it doesn't come out unexpectedly and own us. Observing the stories we make up about other people – and understanding them – teaches us something about our shadow. It means that we can learn who we are and hold less judgment. When we judge another person, it often changes who we are and, interestingly enough, makes us act like them. For example, let's take our person on the train with their feet on the seat. The ego's story was that:

They are disrespectful.
Of course, I am disrespecting their right to be a different person to me. The chances are that I will be sending them some toxic, negative energy, likely to be worse than some shoe dirt.

They don't care about other people.
I don't care about them and I'm likely to make it quite obvious with a disapproving tut or a look.

They are selfish.
It is selfish of me not to think that there might be a very good reason for their feet being up. This might have been the worst day at work, a '16-hours-on-your-feet' shift.

That's the kind of person who doesn't recycle.
I am still thinking about this when I get home and start making dinner. My partner comes home and now I am not in the mood to be loving. I could wipe the aluminum foil clean that I used yesterday and use it again, but as it has a bit of melted cheese on it, I say 'forget it' as I am not in the mood to care, and then I stick it in the landfill trash.

You get my point.

The things that really stick out to us about other people are often the things that we don't like in ourselves. It brings those things out into the open more. Whatever you resist in yourself persists. Often it persists by you witnessing it in other people.

Intuitively knowing who you are and how you become triggered by other people's actions is a valuable tool for transformation. Just don't let the ego turn this into you being a bad person. There is no good and bad. As with the inner observer, it is possible to witness this, laugh about it, and move on. The more focused you become, the deeper it dwells within you. Of course being the witness sometimes means we have to apologize when we screw up. Getting it wrong and being wrong in other people's eyes is okay. True and firm friendships are not built by being nice to each other all of the time. They are built by being authentic and apologizing when you get it wrong. If the friendship breaks under your authentic self then you were not with someone who could hold and witness you. Of course, I am not excluding kindness; we need to be kind, but not create pseudo-friendships. You can have as many of those in one lifetime as you like, but a deep connection comes from your authentic self.

Being authentic is different from telling the truth. The truth can hurt people and be used as a line of defense for hurting people. Being authentic is about taking *ownership* of what bugs you about the other person because you know inside it is really about you, and not so much about them. I am not saying it is okay to be walked over by anyone, and I am aware that being a nice person does seem to give license to those who would be in the ego and abuse a good nature. It would be our ego to allow that abuse; we abuse others when we let them believe it is okay to abuse us. It might be a difficult conversation, but 'no it's not okay with me' said in love has its own healing quality.

How other people affect you

One of the most gratifying human experiences is to connect with another human in a deep and meaningful way. Who we open up to in this way will rely largely on how we connect with someone vibrationally. Some people are a match to our personal theme tune and some people are not. As you get older, your theme tune becomes more defined and you fit in less with everybody else. However, the great thing about getting older is that you stop caring so much about fitting in.

Many things can cause a matching theme tune: a point of view, life experience, cultural background, similar upbringing, your values, your age, even whether you are a positive or negative thinker. All reptiles and mammals share a part of the brain which causes the 'reptilian response,' which drives self-protection, making us run away, stand and fight or freeze (remember the four Fs from chapter 2). When you meet someone that you are not a vibrational match with, you will physically want to move away from him or her.

You'll know this is true if you've ever tried to get an insect to walk onto a piece of paper so you can put it outside the house. You might have witnessed a shift in the insect when it has a moment of realization that there is something wrong with the energy of the paper. It moves backward and then starts running. You couldn't know what the insect is thinking or even see a facial expression. Even when it is frozen still, you can feel its awareness of the danger it is in. How? We are all tuned into energy.

When we are at work, school, or on public transport, we often don't get a choice about our proximity to the energy of others. This can make us feel uncomfortable. It then seems to make common sense that we need some kind of energy protection. However seeking protection makes us vulnerable to the very thing that we are trying to protect ourselves against.

Imagine if negativity sounded like a trumpet and positivity sounded like a flute. You get on a bus playing the sound of a flute and you have to sit close to someone who sounds like a trumpet; let's go as far as saying they are having a really bad day, so an out-of-tune trumpet! You think to yourself that in order to stop this trumpet drowning out your flute, you need some protection around you. The very idea of protection is a negative belief that this trumpet is going to affect your energy and possibly mess up your whole day.

However, in that very moment, you have created negativity and started to sound like a trumpet. By thinking you need protection you buy into the idea that the trumpet can affect you, giving your power to it and, indeed, the trumpet player. You are a beautiful flute, high-pitch loving resonance; you don't even need to play louder for your sound to be heard even over the most out-of-tune of trumpets. Your judgment against it puts you into alignment with it. You might find that becoming intuitively curious means there may be an opportunity for you here; there may even be a reason why this person is offensive to you. Often the people we find most annoying are the ones from whom we learn the most.

That doesn't mean you need to go poking them to find the answer. It is often just a reflection of yourself, of what you fear, that is keeping you away from love. Some people are just so embedded into the story and drama of their situation that there isn't much you can do for them by being in their company. As I discussed earlier, from my perspective the person is in a holding point while they are waiting for more information to guide them to realization. It doesn't mean, however, that I abuse them by making them feel their energy is acceptable to me. They stand no chance of growth from our connection that way. When put in a position where you are energetically going to be tipped from being in alignment with love, you can only set your intention to connect with love and find it any way you can.

The human condition (ego) likes to group together in tribal situations, such as work or places of education. Yet if there is one person whom a member of the tribe finds difficult, the ego will try and get other tribe members to turn against them by complaining about, dehumanizing, and excluding them. You might remember this from being at school, one person in a group of friends falls out with another and the whole group will turn against one, rather than divide. It becomes hard to see the innocent party, if there is one.

Tune in to others

One way to deal with this is to tune in to the root of the person's vibration. This means tuning in to the sound they are creating and making it your sound for a limited time. Another way of putting it would be to 'stand in someone else's shoes.' But how do you do this?

To start with, become curious about the person, then feel them as if they were you. You might feel their tangled web of paranoia, but then underneath there is insecurity and further below there is fear. However, if at first glance all you can see is a horrible person then you have still made a breakthrough. Don't stay at that vibration too long. Just long enough to understand why it is affecting you and its root cause. This can enable you to have compassion for the other person. You might find a very murky aura due to many letdowns in life. You might find you have fallen into their belief about the world from a murky perspective. Having understanding can transcend that person's energy.

Doing this means you are less likely to start acting toward them in the same way that they act toward you, or adding to the critics who end up strengthening that person's negative beliefs about their life story. This is the opposite of what is usually taught about psychic/energy projection, but it is a transformative viewpoint.

Of course, your energy can be leaked day to day by where you focus your attention. The more you give your attention to what is wrong in your life, the more you drain your energy instead of refilling your life with gratitude or joy. The best form of protection from your energy leaking in this way is simply not to buy into what you are being told is a problem. Problems seem really big in the moment. But they are a very important way to learn, so if the problem gives you an opportunity to expand and grow, how can it truly be a problem? Moaning can be good – it bonds people; just don't buy into its importance, as the chances are it's not very important at all. Keeping these things in balance means we can live with people and still grow to be the best of ourselves, while not holding anyone else accountable for how fast we grow.

You in time and space

While we're on the subject of tuning in to energy, living intuitively means being aware of both your own and other people's energy, and this can be a particularly useful skill for city life. This has another name; it is called 'spatial awareness', and when I was trained in theater work the tutors talked a lot about it. It should be common sense to be aware of what is going on around your body but common sense is often anything but common. You may have come across people stopping dead in the middle of a pathway to check a text, or walking really slowly right in the middle of the space so that no one else can get past, or people who board a train and stop in the doorway, or groups of people who block a path like they have become one organism. The list could go on and on, and it's clearly annoying, but all these things are not so much indications of 'the stupid,' but more about people who are in their head rather than in their body. If you notice, whenever it happens, it is usually when someone is in their head and thinking – often in places like the subway or in a grocery store where people are thinking about meals. Often it is when a person is overwhelmed and doesn't know where they are going. When we live in a mixture of our logic and our body we are living in a combination of our mind and our intuition. This way, we can navigate and also have spatial awareness.

Here are some things to look out for in terms of changes in your body. If someone comes up quickly behind you, you will feel a spiky, prickly sensation on the part of your body in a direct line to them. This is a good indicator to move out of the way. If someone is in your way you can 'flash' him or her with a burst of energy, a bit like using high beam when you're driving. In nature, animals and insects are given colors to warn off predators and, with intention, our aura can change color the same way. If you imagine yourself to be the same colors as a wasp, you may find people avoiding you without being aware of why. On other days it is almost as if you don't exist and no one seems able to see you. This is caused by what I call a 'small day.'

Small days happen when you're not feeling good about yourself. The reason for this is that your aura is staying close to your body to give you a thicker layer of protection. This also happens when we are in a place with lots of people, such as a city. If the aura isn't standing out from the body, we don't feel people as they approach. To the 'I'm in a hurry' city dweller, we become a problem. We may even get barked at, as the hurrying person thinks we have no spatial awareness. Having attention in the body and the mind will mean that we are safer as we have awareness of what is going on around us. You don't have to have a large, standout aura for this, you simply become aware of how your aura changes within an environment. If you are in the moment, connecting to the now, you are connecting to yourself in this time and space.

Short days

An ex-boyfriend, Fraser, once commented that I have 'short days' where I look smaller than I am, and 'tall days.' I found this amusing, so I would ask him what height I was on various days. I found that his observations where dependent on my level of self-confidence. I was seen by him to be taller on confident days. As I am 5 feet, 3 inches tall, and he was 6 feet, 2 inches, I worked hard on my self-confidence to be taller.

No need for garlic for energy vampires

We are about to enter into what I would describe as a difficult conversation. I believe it is difficult because our thoughts match frequencies. So if I have a worrying thought, my frequency matches the thing I am worried about. I don't believe this will cause whatever I'm worried about to happen, but it does bring my frequency 'down to its level.' As I told you earlier, I have been using my intuition my whole life and it was only when people started to talk to me about the negative side of energy work that I actually felt any yucky or harmful energy.

However, the ego and the pain-body do love drama; they have a profound ability to make something very simple into something very sinister. So, rather than telling you the popular belief about negative energy, spirit attachments, thought forms and energy parasites, I will tell you what I believe to be true. This will hopefully negate all the fear that the pain-body wants to lap up, and remove another way of it stopping you making progress.

Like attracts like; you have to be in alignment with a negative vibration frequency for it to affect you. So, if you are in alignment with fear, you can attract what you fear. If you believe that negative entities can attach themselves to your aura and drain you of energy then that is what you will attract. It is true what they say about vampires – they can't come in unless you invite them.

So do these negative energy parasites exist? The truth is they don't, unless you give them permission to exist. You give them permission by giving them energy. Here's how it works. Energy can't be created or destroyed, but it can be transformed. Say you heard a story as a child that scared you. Your fear now becomes energy. Perhaps one of your school friends told you about the bogeyman under the bed. That night, you lay awake in bed trying to tell yourself, 'it's all nonsense,' but you still couldn't bring yourself to look under the bed. After a few nights, you could feel the energy of the bogeyman under the bed. Why? The energy you created made a thought form of the bogeyman.

You think of all the people in the world and all the stories of monsters, demons, and vampires. All that energy goes somewhere. The vibration of that energy is of a heavy and dark frequency. If you are tuned to the light and love frequency, you won't even know it exists, until someone tells you. Now, if you know you are in the love frequency, it is the same as me telling you that in a remote island of 'Wombwomb,' they eat babies. Well you're not a baby and you can't even find Wombwomb on a map, so it's likely just a story and has nothing to do with you. Some people try and create the fear in your mind of the Jin spirit, negative energy, curses, etc., to screw with your life and often to charge you money. Knowing that you're not a vibrational match is important.

Belief is a powerful thing

Whatever you believe, you become a match with, and whatever you don't believe, you are disconnected from. I once had a client who found a voodoo object in her husband's wedding jacket, when she took it in to be cleaned, three years after their wedding day. They were happily married for those three years, but hit a disaster after she found the object. I think they wouldn't have had a problem if she hadn't discovered the object. There are many strange and wonderful things in the world. The only way you can fully 'protect' yourself is not to believe that you need protection. Just carry on being happy and trust yourself to be able to handle life and everything it can throw at you.

We are one, but we are not the same

The general spiritual viewpoint is that all humanity is one. I believe that we are all one, but we are not the same. The irony of this is that it somehow seems politically incorrect to make an observation that there is such a thing as racial difference. However, to be in denial about racial difference is to deny a person's identity. The places where you have lived shape you. The origins of your ancestors and parents shape you. In fact, it also becomes a part of the sound you send out into the world – your personal rhythm of life.

The vibration of the food you eat, the star constellations you live under, and the geopathic patterns of the Earth all shape you. The more you live in different countries, the more fragmented you can feel. This often means that you become stronger as a person, but it can make you feel a little isolated as you play a number of different identities, which each have their sound. Humanity seems to be blending its vibration more as we travel, live in other countries, and have more children of mixed race. It's exciting to wonder what the sound of humanity will be like in another ten years.

When you are working with intuition, you can identify the countries a person has lived in by the sound and sound mix they are sending out in their vibration. Tuning in to the difference means that you might be more compassionate when you find a vibration that is a mismatch to your own. There is no such thing as a 'right' sound; we are all different to one another. Understanding the vibrational difference intuitively will help combat racism. Expecting everyone to be the same, and then finding out that they are not, causes a feeling of 'us and them.' Vive la différence for today; with time we are likely to find ourselves blending and harmonizing our individual sound.

Life is difficult: aligning with love

The first self-development book I ever read was M. Scott Peck's *A Road Less Traveled*. He starts the book with these sentences:

> *'Life is difficult. This is a great truth, one of the greatest truths. It is a great truth because once we truly see this truth we transcend it. Once we truly know that life is difficult – once we truly understand and accept it – then life is no longer difficult. Because once it is accepted, the fact that life is difficult no longer matters.'*

This was an influential book in my development. The idea that you could transcend your emotions by accepting what you are struggling with was a revelation. It doesn't mean that life is difficult and you become passive and do nothing, just that it is 'difficult' and being angry only makes it more so.

Being human hurts from time to time. In fact, more often than not being human is difficult. It is difficult because we feel guilty about the state of the world. We feel that we are to blame and yet at the same time we feel helpless to make the necessary changes. Being separate and alone can bring forward many negative emotions.

- Being alone can make us feel: agitated, uneasy, restless, troubled, confused, ambivalent, disconnected, withdrawn, sad, despairing, devastated, discouraged, heartbroken, hopeless, and lonely.

- When we have our personal space, however, we can experience many peaceful emotions: calm, content, satisfied, relaxed, and still.

- Being in unsupportive company can make us feel: frustrated, mortified, annoyed, exasperated, impatient, irritated, aggrieved, hurt, apprehensive, panicked, suspicious, terrified, worried, anxious, nervous, vulnerable, and helpless.

- Most positive emotions are found when we are in supportive company: affectionate, friendly, loving, openhearted, hopeful, grateful, appreciated, interested, curious, fascinated, happy, confident, excited, joyful, playful, adventurous, alive, and expansive.

Looking at the lists of emotions, most of them can be transcended by the same level of acceptance that M. Scott Peck refers to in his statement 'life is difficult.' When we accept how we feel, we transcend the feeling. If we don't accept it, we are more likely to focus on the believed course of our emotions. If that is another person, we are tempted to bend them out of shape to make them see how they are making us feel. We have a choice to transcend through acceptance or to blame others.

Often what allows us to accept an emotion is finding the internal reason for the emotion, and not the external cause. Often the external cause is merely a catalyst to bring up the emotion, to show you how you are out of alignment with love.

When it doesn't fit

I used to work in theater as a stage manager. I loved working on shows and the job was a big break for me into stage-managing musical theater. I was like an excited Labrador puppy; I just couldn't get enough and stuck my nose into everything. I was employed on a long-running show, with people who had worked in musical theater for years. They were jaded and irritated; unsurprisingly, I was holding up a mirror to what they had lost in their careers. They had lost the joy but, rather than self-reflect, they bullied me. Despite this, I stuck at the job and tried very hard to make it work… and I was furious when I was fired. Yet, using my intuition, I knew I was relieved to be free of that environment. So, what was all the anger about? I had been out of alignment with self-love during my employment. If I had loved myself, I wouldn't have allowed the abuse to continue. It is possible to stay angry at the wrong cause of your anger. Often, this means it is hard to move on. Having an intuitive understanding of yourself, but listening with the intuitive mind, means you can understand your triggers so much better. You can't change a whole theater company; you can only move on if something isn't a fit for you.

. . . .

Very bad things happen in life. Life is difficult for many, but for some it can be impossible. Those of us who are sensitive can be deeply affected by the situations that go on in the world. The more awake you become, the more aware you are of the suffering of others. In the *sleeping* world, the media saturation of acts of violence, despair, hunger, and torture have become so commonplace that people just don't feel it. The pain-body almost seems to enjoy it. It's like those people who just have to look at the traffic accident, rather than protecting the safety of passengers in their car by keeping focused on what's ahead. The overwhelming feelings cause us to shut down. This is something to be mindful of, when opening up your intuition. Too open can feel like too much. However, knowing that we can transcend those emotions means that we can remain open and allow the feelings to flow into transformation, rather than allowing them to become stuck.

Out of grace...

There are some events, however, that are impossible to transcend simply by believing that 'life is difficult.' We can reach a point in life when we feel we are at an *impasse* yet somehow even in the most difficult of situations, grace comes from out of nowhere. Natural disasters are one example: we see the devastation, and then a child is pulled out of the rubble. But perhaps one of the hardest things we humans have to deal with – and one of the most impossible ones for us to understand – is man's inhumanity to man, animals, and the environment.

Call to action

I've had the privilege to know two people who were deeply affected by atrocities against civilians – the attacks on 9/11 and the bombing of the London Underground on 7 July 2007.

One of my students was on that train. She felt that she was meant to be there. As the carriage filled with smoke, her intuition told her that she was going to be okay, so she spent her time giving Reiki healing to other shocked and injured passengers. She said it felt better to help. This is a unique perspective, one that helped her to cope. Most people think 'why me?' rather than thinking that they are exactly where they need to be at the time of a devastating incident.

Another woman watched from her window as the first plane hit one of the twin towers in New York. She called 911 and reported what she had seen as she watched the second plane hit. Over the following hours she witnessed firsthand the horrors that many people only witnessed on TV. Afterwards, her way of coping was to help. Over the next few months, she cooked and delivered food, clean socks, and underwear to the firefighters and volunteers who were tasked with recovering the dead from the rubble. It seems the way in which we live through events like these, depending on our lives and experience of loss, is to join together in community to help put things right.

Becoming a hero

As we move toward the shift of consciousness it is likely, due to the dualistic nature of the world, that things will get worse before they get better. It seems that things need to swing into the opposite of what we want until they swing toward our real, loving nature. The only way we can fight these events is with love. I don't mean waving flowers and singing about peace, but an active manifestation of the way we really want things to be. You then no longer become the victim of your situation; you transcend it into becoming the hero.

The perpetrators of such terrorist acts are, of course, so deep in ego that they may not be able to see what they are doing. Or they may have lost all connection with love as a universal force, and can only love and protect from a limited perspective. Many people do things in the name of ego love, which isn't love at all. Just as there can't be a lie where there is truth, looking at a person's action with an analytical mind will not result in understanding. The only thing we can truly hope to understand is the emotion of fear and how it drives us to do things that cause more problems than are solved. The details behind the ego action can only make sense to the damaged ego. Being awake can sometimes feel like talking to a drunken person when you are sober.

Self-development isn't sustainable without community and friends. No matter how much personal work you do on yourself, if you don't have good people around you, you will sink emotionally. We simply can't survive without each other. Of course, people annoy us, hurt us, and disappoint us, but intuition gives us the opportunity to read beyond the ego, to understand why we are hurt, and the reason behind the perpetrator's actions. The ego will always jump to something far more malicious than reality.

I would also go so far as to say that the problems that face humanity could be solved if we come together in community. I'm not kidding! Coming together and listening to each other fully could solve all of our practical problems. But we don't because secretly we're scared of each other. We want to join in community with some people, but not others. We want to lead or follow, but not be too involved or be fully embedded in it. All this is the ego at play. If we could use intuition, we would stop fearing each other and take the necessary steps to make good our communities.

Even global issues could be solved with a global community, using intuition to think differently about our problems, by using the right hemisphere of the brain, which sees things as a whole. We could then communicate using intuition for listening.

This might sound like an idealistic view, but as we move forward I will explain why I believe this might just be possible.

TUNING IN TO WHAT YOU KNOW

- To listen intuitively means to be able to know when you are hearing another person's fear/ego; sometimes just holding a space for them is enough.

- We are not alone but we choose whether or not we go out into the community and use our intuitive knowing and love for the greater good.

- Belief is a powerful force, so don't give negative forces power over you by giving them energy or create 'bad' energy for yourself by listening to other people's stories.

- We have a choice to transcend our emotions by acceptance or blaming others. Often what allows us to accept an emotion is finding the internal reason for the emotion, rather than the external cause. Often the external cause is merely a catalyst to bring up the emotion, to show you how you are out of alignment with love.

Chapter 6
WAKING UP
TO LIVING INTUITIVELY

To live by intuition and heart-based decisions is to live in freedom. It doesn't make for a life without pain and disappointments, as life is still made up of other people living through ego, but what it does give is a greater understanding. In the main, the ego will make up a story about other people's actions, and one that fits its own agenda. Living with intuition is the closest we can get to living with a bit more wisdom. Living intuitively is a work in progress. We have to use our logical mind with intuition; we have little choice in that, but intuitively understanding the world around us and ourselves will lead to a wonderful life based on curiosity and a deepening connection.

Intuitive living starts with intuitively knowing yourself: knowing the influence society has upon you, knowing the influence of your environment, and intuitively being able to hear the universe. We are part of all of these things and need to intuitively feel our connection to everything. The world is changing rapidly, and intuition is one of the major factors in this time of change. If we want to interact from a loving consciousness, we have to change how we understand one another. Intuition is communication without ego.

Knowing about yourself, *knowing* yourself

It's really useful to know about yourself. You can then understand what limits you, what stimulates you, what will make you happy, what challenges you, and what enables you to grow. You can then also talk about yourself: your life, your past, the decisions you made, your plans for the future. These aspects make up your personality, your values, your boundaries, and your dreams. This is self-awareness.

Thinking about ourselves in a navel-gazing way can only take us so far into knowing who we are. In fact, we decide who we are from the information we discover. If you had no experience of life and the world, and you were in an empty room, how would you know who you were? If something entered the room like a dog, you would see yourself in relation to the dog: 'The dog is furry and I am not.' If a child entered the room, it would give you a sense of age and you might find a shift in your emotions and perspective. We know who we are in relation to what we are not. This is one of the many reasons why the people who annoy us the most are often our best teachers. We know about ourselves through our contradiction to and alignment with other people.

Often the reason people feel most alive when they are traveling is because by experiencing other cultures we learn about our own. We know that our environment has created much of who we are. People who live in many different countries may find themselves having personalities that shine differently depending on their environment. All of these personalities are still the real us. Often, when someone dies, we feel a part of us has died with him or her. The person we were when in their company, and the sound we made when we blended our vibration with a person we cared about doesn't die with them, but lives somewhere inside of us. When we look at photos, we can still hear the tune of the union we had with them. In short, who we are in our personality is ever changing and growing, but how does it start?

Understanding your decisions

We make decisions about who we are from childhood, by information we are given about ourselves: 'Good child,' 'bad child,' 'achiever,' 'non-achiever' – it becomes hard to sidestep these roles, as they become the foundation of our personal information. However, once you get adult eyes it is worth looking back and questioning some of the information you were given. Every human being judges another by the perception filter of their experience, including your parents. If you have a mother with low self-esteem, she isn't going to believe that a child born from her is going to grow up and be a genius. She might even want to protect that child from ridicule and limit the child's options in life so they aren't disappointed. No one ever actually thinks anything about you. No thought can ever fully be about you. It is always going to be put through the perception of the ego.

People who like you do so because you fit into their needs or values. People who don't like you often find that something about you triggers that dislike, which can be jealousy or even seeing something in you that makes them dislike themselves. This means that no one can tell you who you are, but you can learn who you are by witnessing yourself in their presence: how you react to situations and what emotions come up for you.

Breaking out of old patterns

Your sub-personalities can block some of these emotions by taking the form of a family member or teacher from your younger days. In school reports, I was described as 'lazy, must try harder.' I struggled terribly at school and the result of the struggle was that I gave up. I am not at all lazy and I don't know many people who try as hard as I do; I just didn't get the support I needed. However, taking this belief about myself into adulthood formed me into a workaholic, strapped between the sub-personalities of the critic and the controller. Intuitive knowing allows us to look at information that has been presented to us and to see if we resonate with it.

Be your authentic self

When you look at yourself through the curiosity of intuitive eyes, you start to see yourself more authentically. You are able to feel the sound vibration of what you believe you are, from what people have told you in the past; and who you are, based on your actions and how you show up in life. People often talk about what 'resonates' with them in something they hear or read. What they are describing is what makes a sound that complements their authentic knowing. Some people feel that resonance often, and some people never feel it. You can resonate with something you know to be true, whether or not you have direct experience of the subject matter. The more you develop intuitively, the more your ability to have an accurate picture of who you are emerges.

It is worth having a spring clean of the ideas you have about yourself that are based upon what other people have told you. You can do this by listening intuitively to yourself every time you get triggered into a negative emotion. Current emotions resonate sharply; old emotions are dull. You might compare this to the pain experienced when having a massage – old, tight muscles or injury have a dull pain and new pain is sharp. Intuitively hearing your resonance means that you will know if someone in the current moment has hurt your feelings or if this old pain, which is causing you to react. If it's old pain, it is worth checking in intuitively with how you really feel before reacting from an old space. From a very early age, we were trained to shut down our original responses to the stimuli of life. For example, statements such as, 'What's wrong?' when we show an emotion that is not seen to be positive, or 'Don't be scared' or 'You're being silly.' We are talked out of our feelings and when we are young we take in this entire information. We make it part of our life map of the way we must behave in society.

Accepting who you are

One of the saddest things we can do is to medicate our emotions, not allowing ourselves to feel authentically whatever we are feeling. This is especially true when children are medicated because an adult can't cope with the child's energy. I am not saying that all medication isn't needed; I'm not a medical doctor. However, I have seen too many people put on medication when what they actually needed was to find a space to be in touch with their feelings. When the Earth goes into winter we don't think there is something wrong and it should be in spring and summer *all* the time. Like winter, being sad and reflective is when we nurture the seeds of our renewal. In the same way, it is okay to be thoroughly miserable from time to time.

When we intuitively know ourselves authentically, we act and react differently. This can burst abusive or unloving relationships, allowing us to find authentic, deep love and to build firm foundations in our business/career communication. Knowing yourself by what you intuitively resonate with means that you know yourself from your heart. Knowing from your head is based in past 'learning' and not the 'knowing' of 'you' in the present. By doing this, we also start to change our story. It is never about what has happened to us that is important; it is about what we made those events mean that affects our future the most. As, in order to be right about our perceptions, we replay them in the drama of our life, gaining more evidence that our limiting beliefs are correct. When we know if we resonate with the story in this present moment, it means we can move through its holding pattern.

Intuitive living starts with showing up to life from your authentic self. It takes some intuitive awareness and mindfulness, but the blessing is the feeling of being set free to choose from the heart and not just the head. The responsibility of intuitive knowing isn't just using what you know, but adapting how you communicate with others. When you see past someone's fear into the root cause of why they are afraid, you can acknowledge it and do nothing about it or you can choose to help undo the tightness of the knot around their story, by not playing a character. You can respond from a loving place, inspiring the person to do the same. Of course, I am not saying be taken advantage of, but occupy the higher ground toward love, which can transform fear. When you move past a fear in this lifetime, it never presents itself in another life. You have mastered that part of ego and moved on from it as a lesson point. Isn't that a great gift to give others? One by one it shifts humanity.

Hearing your music as you dance

Our body is a wonderful indicator of the world around us. Intuition is the way to reawaken your natural and authentic responses to the energy of other people and the world. As we have discussed, everything that exists vibrates, therefore everything that exists makes a sound. Your body and its energy system are sensitive to these sounds. The trick is to be able to interpret the sounds into information. The sound vibration information may be interpreted as emotions, pictures, feelings, symbols, etc. This level of understanding might be enough to 'know' without the words. However, if you need to communicate what you know then the left hemisphere of the brain will have to turn the information into words.

One way of accessing what the body knows is to allow your body to work through your imagination. We don't often think of the body itself being inspired, but the body can be inspired – this is what happens when we dance. The body is constantly moving without the brain making conscious decisions to tell it to move, like blinking our eyes for example. Anyone who has had to learn a dance routine will know that if you think about the steps your feet have to make, you will find it difficult; but once you know the steps, the best thing to do is let the body move and stop thinking about them. You also find that when a musician plays music you can see the energy running through them. So, next time someone catches you dancing in the living room when you thought you were alone, grab them by both hands and swing them round the room.

Shamans have used drumming for thousands of years as a way to bring forward information for the tribe. Music can induce all kinds of trance-like states, which allow the right hemisphere of the brain to see useful images. Letting the body move in a space or interpret the sound through the imagination can be very powerful.

There are two ways in which music can help you develop your intuition. One is to allow the right hemisphere of the brain to open and have downloads of information. (You may remember that language functions are located in the left brain, but music lives over on the right side of the brain.) The other way is to open the body and its energy systems to bring forward *somatic* knowing. In this way, we can also unlock emotions held in the physical body, which might be holding us back in our past; they might be an aspect of the pain-body and not allow us to flow into happiness in our present moment.

Knowing without words

To experience who you are at your deepest essence is to know yourself without words, to know that part of you which is without form. For example, you can't know God with words. To know who you are with words is to limit you. The part of you that is the unformed, beyond comparison being – probably you can't even think about it because the mind cannot conceive it. The only connection you have with it is that of inner knowing. To know yourself with intuitive eyes is to recognize a timeless and formless consciousness. You might know it in a second and lose the connection; you might feel it for a while and wish that you could keep it. Intuitively knowing this part of you is easy to do in a room alone but much harder to keep connected in the community, when people bring you back to your ego.

Yet, when you know it – when you have felt the *real* you – it is a place that you can remind yourself is there, and it makes it easier to let go of the importance that ego places on life. This inner knowing is breathing as one with the breath of life and death and knowing that we are energy. We are one and connected; at that level of knowing, none of the everyday matters we concern ourselves with are truly important. I don't wish to trivialize how painful and difficult life can be, but it is our perception that makes it hard. Going with the flow is like dancing on breath; the ego can't hold you, and your spirit is free.

I have no words to share with you. It is an impossible thing to connect with through words, as it has no words. I can't tell you how to find it, as this will force you more deeply into ego. Life gives you the pointer to find it. Other teachers can give you pointers to find it but ultimately, when we stop looking at the finger for direction, we feel it: it, the finger, the heart, the breath, and, at the same time, none of these things at all.

Addiction and sedation

Part of the problem we can have with tuning in to our knowing is that we are not ourselves and 'sedate' ourselves to what is going on around us. Call your therapist, call your sister, call a cab, call who you want, I'll give you your number so you can call yourself, – the chances are you do have an addiction. Now, where's my coffee?

Addiction is a huge problem that is holding humanity back from making change. Living intuitively means we can wake up to our addictions in the search for happiness. Addiction isn't solely about being dependent on drugs or alcohol; we are also held back from our spiritual evolution through addiction. The main reason is that most addictions keep us sedated or in a cycle of dependence, which keeps us in a holding pattern. It is possible for us to become addicted to *anything* that makes us feel better. Addictions can range from a basic sugar rush or buying something new, to not letting go of a relationship, right the way through to social standing, power, and control. We can even become addicted to our spiritual beliefs, making us believe that we are living a better and more righteous life than others. When we become hooked on something, no matter how loud our intuitive knowing, it can't break through to help us make a decision to change.

Going places

I was once what I call a 'cappuccino woman.' I'd buy a coffee, luxury skinny latte or a cappuccino and make my way onto the subway. Overtaking tourists and doing a do-si-do around fellow commuters I would rush. *Coming up on the far side, clearing the first ticket barrier, it's cappuccino woman in the lead, one more furlong to go before the tricky escalators. Is she walking? Yes she is, it's cappuccino woman walking up the escalators. She WINS... cappuccino woman has won the commuter race, not a drop of coffee spilt.* It is what's known as 'hurry up and wait' as I am usually early for everything. The rush made me feel as if I was important. Why I didn't get a coffee when I got where I was going, I have no idea. I was too busy being important for common sense! This is addiction to self-importance... and coffee.

Behaviors

We unknowingly fall in and out of addictions throughout our lifetime. Some are harmless and some can become hooks that make it hard for us to follow our intuition. We feel safe when we live in patterns; these patterns in themselves can become addictive. Sometimes we believe we are heading in the right direction only to find that we are going round in circles. The cause of this 'need' for addiction comes from the different experiences of our day-to-day lives. An individual isn't always fully responsible for their addictive behavior. It can also be the mass consciousness of the environment that holds them locked into a pattern of being. Take a walk through any train station in any city and you will have instructions barked at you over the public-address system: 'Mind the gap' and 'Do not leave bags unattended.' None of us really like being told what to do. You then see the faces of your fellow commuters, but never their eyes, some with their noses deep in a free newspaper that's giving them more things to worry about and more instructions.

Then, from the corner of your eye, you catch a smiling face – she's holding a bottle of perfume, she has perfect hair and perfect make-up; another poster letting you know that happiness depends on what you own and not who you are. The TV tells you how to lead a perfect life while the media brings down anyone who falls off the pedestal, into his or her shadow, or is photographed falling out of a taxi while drunk. In cities across Europe and the USA, you see men and women, coffee in hand, making their way into work – coffee, their necessary prop for looking successful and busy.

All the energy that drives our needs and wants is masculine energy. Masculine and feminine – or male and female energy – has little to do with being a man or a woman. The masculine energy is in line with the logic of the left brain. It brings a vibration linked with 'doing, fixing, sorting, and achieving.' The feminine energy brings a vibration of 'receptive, stillness, reserving, and being.' When we feel as if we are lacking in our life, we turn to the masculine energy; we feel there is something that needs to be fixed, something outside of who we are. If we feel that we are not enough, so we look for something to make us feel better. The ego also resonates better with the masculine energy. The ego allows us to put ourselves first, so that we make sure we have safety, food, and shelter. Happiness found outside of you is only *temporary*; inner happiness is permanent, but it kills off part of the ego self. The ego fools you into believing that happiness is only outside of you, so that the ego false self can continue to exist. Your intuition can let you know the difference between listening to your head and the information you are led to believe is true, as opposed to what your heart knows *is* true.

Your heart knows you have enough of everything you need; your ego will always tell you that you will be happy sometime in the future when you have the things you want. This leads to more wanting and addiction, the chasing of which keeps you from the things that really matter.

Drugs

Let's take a look at drug addiction. Addicts are often very sensitive people. They've fallen down a gap between reality and our common perception of it, unsurprisingly feeling that they don't fit in with the world. Their drug of choice will also represent the imbalance in their masculine and feminine energy. Looking at recreational drugs, we see they are linked to the 'uppers,' which make you feel high, happy and able or 'downers,' which make you feel numb or distant.

Hash, heroin, ketamine, and diazepam are all downer drugs, but also feminine energy (receptive, stillness, reserving, and being). Cocaine, ecstasy, amphetamines, and crack are upper drugs, but also masculine energy (doing, fixing, sorting and achieving). Rebalancing the energy that is lacking or finding other ways to bring the energy in can really help fight addiction.

 Find another way

A friend smoked hash every day because he didn't like himself when he was aggressive or male dominant. He smoked pot as it brought out his feminine side, which he much preferred. He was an artist and he felt that the creative energy of the right, female side of the brain was helping him. Sadly, however, the feminine energy of 'receptive, stillness, and being' meant that he didn't have the necessary male drive to get any work done. His relationships failed and he wasn't marketing his artwork, which he needed to do in order to generate income. A better method would have been to allow the feminine within him to emerge without the drugs – perhaps through meditation, which in itself is 'receptive, stillness, and being.' Another friend who was a crack and heroin addict had to mix the two to balance the male and female essence of the drugs, also known as the upper and downer.

Food

Even food has an addictive quality. When I gave up gluten I went through withdrawal. My emotions crashed and I felt really depressed for about two weeks. It wasn't simply due to lack of cheesecake. I knew what was happening so I could go along with it. However, you can see why changing diet is so hard for people. Foods with carbs and sugar are addictive, and giving them up will make you feel lousy for a while. But if you're intolerant of those foods, they will weigh your energy down. Getting the right diet can make you feel like you're flying, once you get it right.

Breaking free

When breaking any addiction, you must understand that you are not 'your thoughts.' You are the thinker of your thoughts. Many people feel that they are linked to their addiction because they can hardly think of anything else except the things that they crave most. The thinker has the ability to control those thoughts. The key to an addiction-free life is to balance your male and female energy, have a tamed ego and try to face all fear head on. That way fear never becomes the theme by which you resonate. This means that you can keep a loving consciousness when all around you might be resonating with fear.

There is another aspect of us that can never be addicted: our awareness or 'observer' – the part of us that is also devoid of emotions. When you are panicking, the awareness isn't panicked. When you become angry you are aware that you are angry, but the awareness is calm. This is also true when it comes to alcohol or drugs. You can be very drunk, even slurring your words, yet the awareness is sober. With this being the case, the awareness can't be present within your body or mind, as it would be affected by alcohol. Your awareness is an observer who oversees everything, but has no judgment or connection to it.

Love-based intuition has a strong connection with this part of you. People who study meditation often connect with the 'awareness' self. Once you have found it, you will want to be in that space all the time. Just knowing it is there, and that it is always still and calm, brings a serenity to even the hardest situations. The awareness is never addicted, judgmental or disappointed; the awareness simply 'is.' Some people relate 'being in a state of awareness' to 'being in the moment' (out of the ego), which would make sense, as addiction is the opposite of awakening. Addiction is being sedated. Actor Jim Carrey talked about his feeling of awakening, which was inspired by Eckhart Tolle's work:

> *'Who is it that is aware that I am thinking? And suddenly I was thrown into this expansive, amazing, feeling of freedom, from myself, from my problems. I saw that I was bigger than what I do, I was bigger than my body, and I was everything and everyone. I was no longer a fragment of the universe, I was the universe, and ever since that day, I have been trying to get back there.'*

I couldn't put it better myself. It comes and goes. It's like riding a wave, sometimes I am on, sometimes I am off, but at least I know where I want to go, and I want to take as many people with me as I possibly can because the feeling is 'amazing.'

Intuition in society

Our addiction to 'stuff' is just another indication that for many people Western society simply isn't working and they are just looking for ways to 'get out of it' while staying 'in it.' This was perhaps most clearly illustrated by the riots in the UK in 2011 and the LA riots in 1992. It is easy to blame politics but the simple fact is that capitalism places people at the top and people at the bottom. It's the job of the people at the bottom to try and make it to the top. It is the job of the people at the top to stay there. Someone is always losing and the truth is that in the end everyone loses. We simply can't continue to run business the way we have been doing. Large corporations have more power over governments than we would care to believe.

We know what the problems are – we see them and often live them every day. When you look at society with 'awareness,' it looks like everyone has been drinking water from the well of madness and the person with awareness is the only one left who is normal. Every human has this awareness and knows inside what needs to happen to make the changes we need, but fear often stops us from making those decisions. We feel trapped because unless we all change together at once, the individual finds it too overwhelming to be the only one playing the game without any ego-based rules. Rules don't work; it's only values that can guide behavior and overturn rules for the greater good. Think about some of the famous civil rights activists such as Rosa Banks or leaders such as Mahatma Gandhi who upheld their values, and in so doing overturned the rules.

We have lost our collective values as humans and value power over love because of fear. When we can escape from a society based on fear, we'll have freedom. But you, as an individual, can be free from fear. Intuition is the key. Trust your intuition and you never have to trust another living soul. You will be able to see where other people are coming from. Watching news interviews becomes very different when we watch with intuitive knowing. We are so used to being fed information that we have lost the ability to discern the true facts. Many people feel that they don't understand the information they are being given, so thinking about it doesn't help. Often the information is deliberately confusing. If we really understood it, we might rise up and say 'NO.'

Most of us live in a state of overwork and overwhelm, so it is likely we would understand information fed to us if we only had the energy or the time to put into it. Many people don't vote because they haven't got the opportunity to look into the policies, and they also feel it's pointless because whatever political party gets into power, the plan goes out of the window anyway. Intuition takes seconds to make a decision. I intuitively know if something in the news isn't true or if a politician comes from the same sense of values as myself, but it doesn't go deeply enough into the whole picture. For example, I can hear on the news if someone is telling a lie, but it doesn't mean I know what the truth is behind the lie. However, it is a step in the right direction and better than being in a state of apathy due to having too many other things to deal with in life.

Freedom from being controlled

Who we are as people can fluctuate depending upon the circumstances we live in. This might seem an obvious point, but it is often overlooked in its importance when it comes to judging other people and the power of the sub-personality. We simply don't know who we can become when the circumstances of life change. The Stanford prison experiment in Berkeley, California, is a prime example.

The Stanford Prison Experiment was a study of the psychological effects of becoming a prisoner or prison guard. In 1971, a team of researchers at Stanford University selected students to play the roles of guards or prisoners and live in a mock prison housed in the Stanford psychology building. The results were shocking; participants playing guards adapted to their authoritarian roles and made prison life uncomfortable for the prisoners. The prisoners, even knowing this wasn't a real prison and they could leave, stayed and allowed themselves to be mistreated by fake prison officers.

What we learned from this experiment, and others that followed, was that if you give a person a task, job, role, or position of responsibility the ego can act without any empathy and, in many cases, with extreme cruelty. Tragically, we see these offences against 'other' humans again and again in history and every day in the newsfeed: against women, children, social groups, and people of all creeds and ethnic origin. We tend to dehumanize the perpetrators but in truth, we all have an ego capable of these actions with the right justification.

You might also believe that if you were in a life-and-death situation that you would help others. In fact, you might turn and run. The truth is that we don't fully know who we are. The only thing we can know is that, given the right set of circumstances, we have the capacity to be anyone. That doesn't mean we all have the 'X factor' and people who can't sing can be singers. But if your joy is to share love, through singing, and no one likes your singing, find a new way to share love.

We are all one, but we are not the same. What causes us to be different is the life we were born into and what we have made it mean from one moment to the next. Our ego is happy to play a role when faced with having to be an authority or to respond to authority. We allow authority to shape our lives. This is truer in some countries than in others. Our intuitive knowing gives us the opportunity to seek out the beating drum that we are being told to dance to and to start to see the deeper effects in a situation. In other words, know where your reactions are coming from.

By the same token, when we are faced with people in authority, just like the student prisoners in the Stanford Prison experiment, we often lose our common sense. For example, doctors in the USA have been encouraging families that have relatives suffering with Alzheimer's disease to have them micro-chipped. With society's fear of child abduction, is it only a matter of time before someone suggests that children are chipped in the same way? Good role models are needed from the top down in order for people to give respect to authority. Authority needs to give leadership that empowers others to lead in their community by first being a positive role model.

Puppy love

When I got my dog, she was a small, very cute puppy. The vet told me horror stories about puppies being stolen and taken out of the country. She convinced me to get my dog micro-chipped. In that moment I allowed a large chip to be placed between my dog's ears, so that if she was stolen I had some chance of tracking her and getting her back. My dog squealed with pain as the blood seeped onto her white fur. To be honest, no risk of losing her was worth it. I did it because my ego was triggered by fear. I didn't take any other knowing into account. This was the vet and the vet knew better than I did.

Working with intuition means that you can never be controlled through your fear. It means that you can never be bought or sold in your choices for you or your family. It is a step up, to view a vantage point beyond your ego triggers, to put you back in fearless control over your life.

Intuition for living things

We have mostly talked about intuition for knowing yourself, others, your community, and society but you can also use intuition for reading the natural world around you. Everything that exists has energy and a sound vibration.

In order to learn, we are used to going out and getting information, like collecting data about the world. When we talk of tuning in to anything – be it a person, a blade of grass, or a fish – it is hard for us not to think of it in terms of action. Intuition involves no action; it is to be open to receive and hear what is out there to be heard. If you wanted to intuitively know a fish, you would first enter into a mind state of curiosity about the fish, which forms a questioning energy, 'How can I know you?' Through your curiosity you shift your consciousness toward loving the fish. Your body then opens and starts to form a resonance with the fish. You may feel energy changes in your body; your body starts to know what it is to be a fish.

Okay, so this might sound a little nuts and I deliberately used a fish because we don't tend to feel like we have any resonance to something that lives in water. To help you with this shift of perspective, remember that you are not just a body; you are energy, too. The body is a wonderful receiver of information about what your energy is telling you. Energy knows the fish as energy. All things can know the energy/sound that is in all things. Allowing the knowing to come and avoiding analyzing the knowing is the key. Back to the fish. Your body will start to feel emotions, knowing and sensations that don't feel like your own. You will also note how the fish becomes curious about you. I did this once in the London Aquarium. I ended up with a crowd of people around me as the fish just looked at me and didn't move from the side of the tank, right in front of me. Seriously I do this stuff for fun!

Telepathy is feeling at a distance. What I was feeling from the fish was a sense of taste that the fish has through its scales – because the fish has an awareness of the water, which holds memory. Tuning in I knew that the fish was aware of what it was like to live in an ocean, even though it had only ever lived in captivity. Contrary to my belief that the fish would rather live in the ocean, the fish actually conveyed that it had an understanding of the two lives and felt it was better off in this place. It simply wasn't fond of some of the chemicals in the water it had to swim through, as they didn't taste nice. The fish was making a sound; everything is making sound. Tune in – like a radio – to that sound, and then enable it to enter and change you, in the same way that music can move you and change your emotions.

Animals have an awareness of which humans mean them harm and which don't. I only need to watch my dog. She is totally aware of a person who may want to pet her. I have a very friendly dog, but her instincts about people are never wrong. She won't go up to just anyone or allow anyone to touch her. Animals live on their intuition, as we humans did once.

Intuition for the world

All humans once knew the land; they understood the animals and were part of nature. Intuition was an integral part of human survival. As we drove on in our evolution we forgot the very thing that sustained us – the Earth. We are now at such a point of disconnect with the Earth that we might very well die out as a species, as well as taking many other life forms with us. There are many reasons why we have reached this point but it is now the solutions that must become most important to us. I can't teach you how to hunt, fish, or thrive in a world where the living conditions are now more or less extinct. But I can teach you how to reconnect to the inner knowing that you have forgotten, but not lost. It is one of the most useful survival techniques you can ever know.

For city life it is a case of being very streetwise. It helps you find work and understand the nature of a town or city, or even a building. Intuition allows you to connect with history more fully. For nature, you understand plants, water, animals, and insects with a different level of knowing. It is at this point that the world changes color. You become connected to the physical world and its vibration, as you become a *part* of the whole; rather than feeling you are *on* the Earth, you have the chance to be *with* the Earth.

This is important for right now, but it is also vital for our future survival. We know that our current way of life isn't sustainable, and we are unsure of what will happen in the future. Intuitive knowing of plants and animals could once again be as vital as it is for the few remaining indigenous tribes who live on intuition for their survival. If you want to kill a fish with a spear you can't simply aim at the fish, you need to aim at the next move of the fish. The fish could be a metaphor for all the moves we make in life – don't aim for what you know; aim for what is possible.

This is how we need to restructure the way we work together. When we have to join together in community to survive, or when you have to make decisions where you have no knowledge to rely upon, your inner knowing could be the one thing that saves your life.

Everything is made of vibration, so everything is made of sound, including plants, buildings, water, and the ground itself. You might not be able to hear it with your ears, but you can 'know' it with the whole of you. This knowing is a form of blending your resonance with whatever you are tuning in to and listening to. As everything is made of sound, so nothing is truly physical, which means that you are able to intuitively tune in to everything that exists. As the observer, you can know everything around you and you can even tune in at a distance to everything. Everything that exists is part of one vibration, singing as one. Being part of this immense sound, you can tune in to it as a whole and into individual parts.

The Earth sings. The sound is different during the changing seasons; it is different from one country to the next. Having spent a few years working on cruise ships I have even found that the ocean sings a different song at night than during day. You can feel it; it's tangible. I believe this is how fishermen once understood the sea before technology came along. Everything is made of sound and when you open up your being to intuitively receive, you can hear the Earth in all of its aspects. It isn't more difficult tuning in to the Earth just because it is bigger. Your personal energy is at one with everything else. So this is just a case of plugging into what is already part of you. The same concept applies.

You can't 'know' nature in a conventional sense. You can read guidebooks that will tell you all about a particular building, just as you can get information about a tree or a plant, but the only way to really know something is through your intuitive practice of knowing – inner knowing that is without words. Without this you only conceptualize, draw conclusions, and create limits. Only through your internal experience of it can you know really know the nature of what it is, the very sound and energy of its being.

You might feel a little uncertain about connecting with the planet, as you may worry that you will become overwhelmed with her hardship and pain. However, you are likely to find the opposite to be true. Don't decide in advance what you will feel, allow yourself to feel what you feel. We know that talking to plants makes them grow, and I don't think it is because we breathe out what they breathe in, as my science teacher tried to tell me. It is easy to develop a preconceived idea about what other people are thinking, let alone a plant and, of course, that gives room for the ego to fill in the blanks, before intuition is received.

Connecting with the Earth

I find nighttime is the best time to connect with the Earth, or just after rain when everything is reaching out for the water. Intuition isn't just a gift to be able to hear other humans fully, it is also a way to bring back skills that we once had and have now lost – the ability to hear and know plants and animals. At this time, intuition is a vital aspect of human and world survival. When you understand what something needs and the energy behind all things, you become as one. This form of intuitive blending can cause a very intense feeling of oneness. You can totally lose a sense of yourself and feel a state of bliss. I can't promise you will feel this, but intuitive practice can lead to many levels of awakened consciousness.

You are not alone

But don't fear, you won't be alone in using your newfound skills; your new way of being. And I don't mean if you start communing with nature in public that you'll attract a crowd – although this could happen. No, you won't be alone because if you look around it is easy to find evidence of another world of people rousing themselves and using their intuition. In 2011, Steve Jobs, the 'Apple' chairman and former CEO – who made personal computers, smartphones, tablets, and digital animation mass-market products – died. Soon after his death, many of his quotes were published in social media. One from his now very famous 2005 Stanford Commencement address read:

> *'Don't let the noise of others' opinions drown out your own inner voice. And most importantly, have the courage to follow your heart and intuition. They somehow already know what you truly want to become. Everything else is secondary.'*

And Steve Jobs is not the only successful entrepreneur to see the true value of intuition, as the UK business magnate and chairman of Virgin, Sir Richard Branson, was reported as saying, 'I rely far more on gut instinct than researching huge amounts of statistics,' and Bill Gates, the Microsoft legend who now devotes most of his time to humanitarian causes, said, 'Often you have to rely on intuition.'

I love it, I love it, I love it, I love it and, at the same time, I am also very annoyed! How come when intuition was all about female intuition it was disregarded as hogwash but when men in business admit they've been making money from their intuition for years and years, now everyone is saying what I've been saying for… well… years and years. Still I can't complain because it might be the reason why you have this book in your hands.

The word 'intuitive' has now become a buzzword in technology. People now make requirements of software designers for the 'program to be intuitive:' 'We need an intuitive design,' 'Why isn't the interface intuitive?' User Interface Engineering put it perfectly in one of their blogs:

> *'To those who police the English language, interfaces can't be intuitive, since they are the behavior side of programs and programs can't intuit anything. When someone is asking for an intuitive interface, what they are really asking for is an interface that they, themselves, can intuit easily. They are really saying, "I want something I find intuitive."'*

This is what we look for in our phones, cars, computers, TVs, or any other techy toys. We want easy-to-use technology and we don't want to read the instruction manual. We want to be able to pick it up and it intuitively make sense to us.

However it came about, it still makes me happy that we are now using these words, changing business, and starting to see the importance of honesty and transparency. And while intuition is vital on a global scale, being intuitive each and every day also makes your life easier and means that you'll never be sold a dud car from a used car salesman.

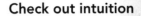

Check out intuition

I was shopping with my mother in one of those megastores, the kind of place I don't usually shop. In the pet department I found an expensive pet food product that I normally buy, discounted to 80 percent of the usual retail price! I am so excited I nearly do an arm sweep across the shelf into the cart. Calming down I take three of one kind and one of another. At the checkout I have braced myself for a more expensive shop than usual but, just as I'm paying, I have a sick feeling in my stomach – something just feels off. When I get home, I check my receipt and discover that only one of the pet products I'd picked up had been reduced. I didn't feel it when I was looking at the shelf of products – I was too busy being excited about my bargain. It's easy to put logic down in your excitement, but don't ignore feelings of unease or curiosity. Look a little deeper and you'll usually see the problem. Just think how useful your intuition might be for those really big purchases, such as buying a house. In fact, I recently pulled out of a house I was buying with my very understanding friend Sam and, at the time, I couldn't fully explain in any logical way why. Only in the months to follow did information unfold in both of our lives that meant this house would have trapped our future growth. Following your intuition at times isn't for wimps, but it makes your life easier in the long run.

Being awake in a sleeping world

So right now, you might be noticing that your life has started to change. It can be tough being awake in a sleeping world. It becomes all too tempting to want to beat a loud drum and wake up others, yet there are many ways in which your increasing lightness of being can help and inspire others, without you breaking into a sweat.

You might also feel like a bit of a space alien, out of connection with other humans. As you remove more blocks, you are changing your dense vibrational energy to one of light; and up the balloon goes. When you are talking to people who are more solid, it is easy to blend your energy with theirs, and have a kind of yo-yo effect. Our default is always the vibration we are most familiar with. As pack animals we want to fit in and not be left out in the cold. Being a person who is conscious on a different level to the rest of humanity can be daunting. Who do you hang out with? Connecting with people on a day-to-day level is tough; authentic connection is even more difficult.

Being a vibrational mismatch to the majority of humanity is hard. But doesn't it feel better? Isn't it what you signed up for, before you were even a glint in your father's eye? If you stick to your lightness of being, often people around you will tune more into you than try to drag you down to their level. It takes practice and an attitude of mindfulness when you do find yourself slipping. Most people who attain enlightenment do it on the side of a mountain, alone, but anyone can be an angel when their feathers are not being ruffled. What is being asked of you is to do it in community. It's not the fastest road, but it is the most sustainable.

Living in a capitalist society, we are governed to think in an egotistical way in order to survive. Your job might demand it of you. Who you have to interact with on a day-to-day basis may demand it of you. The more awake you become, the more you are aware of the people around you who are sleeping. It can sometimes make you feel angry, sad, and disheartened, as if it's all hopeless – and, of course, this is your ego trying to put you back to sleep.

Feed your intuition

In the movie *The Matrix* the lead character, Neo, has a choice of living life in the dream or choosing to wake up. This is a perfect metaphor for the ego's view of life. You can live life believing the stories the ego tells you are real or you can wake up to the 'real you' and live with intuition. Deep inside you wanted to change; deep inside, it wasn't enough for you to live without being authentically alive – because deep inside you knew that there was more to you and much more to life. For you, it's simply never enough. The downside of being awake in a sleeping world is that you are likely to feel more disconnect with the lies that go on around you. Everyone else seems happy with the lie, so you can't wake them up by conversation and that can be frustrating. It can cause pressure on relationships and family; it can make you think that perhaps you're the one who's crazy while the rest of the world 'gets it.' Yet, in contrast to all of that, when you do have connection, it is the most authentic experience you can have, and brings with it the most joy.

There is a Native American parable about a grandfather who says, 'I feel as if I have two wolves fighting in my heart. One wolf is vengeful and angry; the other is loving and compassionate.' When asked which wolf will win the fight in his heart, the old man replies, 'The one I feed.'

The more you feed the ego, the more it wins. The more others try and tip your hand to feed your ego, the more you need to feed the other wolf. How you feed that wolf is up to you. Likeminded friends are a great way to feed the right wolf. When in the presence of people who are not likeminded, sometimes it's just better not to enter into a discussion that will force you into feeding the wrong wolf. It doesn't mean that you agree with what's being said, it just means that you are still and quiet in your authenticity.

TUNING IN TO WHAT YOU KNOW

- Intuitive living starts by knowing yourself: understanding your beliefs and values, and also how you fit into the greater community and universe. Tuning in to all living things, your natural environment – whether that's urban or rural – connects you to the planet.

- The world is changing rapidly, and intuition is one of the major factors in this time of change. If we want to interact from a loving consciousness, we have to change how we understand one another.

- Intuition is communication without ego meaning you can respond from a place of love and empathy to everyone and everything around you – you wake up to your 'real self' and see the 'truth' behind the 'roles' that you and other people play.

- Living intuitively makes you curious about the messages you're given by society and the world at large. Working with intuition means that you can never be controlled through your fear, because intuition opens up your perspective and gives you control over your life.

- Become less skeptical and more curious, and accept that it won't always be easy being awake in a sleeping world but it will probably be more fun.

Chapter 7
INTUITIVE KNOWING OF THE NON-PHYSICAL WORLD

You are the single, most important thing in the whole universe and you are of no consequence whatsoever. Somewhere in between the two is the truth. We give meaning to life and giving spirituality to our life is another way to give our existence meaning. The truth is that our existence might mean nothing, but it might mean everything. Belief that it means nothing comes from the same level of ego as belief that it means everything. Somewhere in the middle is the balance – the breath between the words. The breath may be an in-breath or an out-breath; it is unimportant. What is important is that there is a space before the action of breathing takes place.

If nothing is important then why do we need to bother being spiritual at all? Spirituality is about something that goes beyond life; it's about giving a purpose to your existence as a spirit.

The two selves

Most people don't remember being in the womb, their birth or being very small. This is mainly because we didn't have the language to give our experiences meaning. If I step into another part of my recall mind I can remember the sensations of being in the womb, but it was without conscious thought. When our thoughts become conscious we have reached a certain point in our development. We are no longer just a sponge for information; we give that information meaning. Only then do things start to make sense and the ego mind starts to figure things out. It is possible that we lived in a different form before we were even conceived, but with our current mind we wouldn't remember, as this mind demands the memory to have a meaning.

The things that people generally remember the most clearly are the things that have meaning to them. Of course memory can't be trusted, as we often give meaning to events upon reflection. It is the ego that makes meaning out of life. It is therefore possible that life goes on after death and life went on before you were even a sperm and an egg. Of course the ego hates the very idea of its death and might just be making all this stuff up, but there is another knowing. It is an inner knowing, which knows that we survive the death of the physical body. This inner knowing also directs us to lead a good life. Otherwise, what would be the point of leading a life where at times we painfully take the right road for the greater good of all?

Because we 'know' that we are a part of something much bigger than ourselves. It is not a belief in a judgmental God who is going to cast us out if we don't do as he says. It's a knowing that if there is, in fact, a fight between good and evil then that fight is going on inside of us. Every time we choose love in our lifetime it is one small victory for our collective higher consciousness.

Each one of us is really two selves, locked into a perpetual arm-wrestling contest. Both sides keep lifting their elbows off the table, and accusing the other side of cheating.

Removing the blocks

Life is about removing the blocks we have created with the ego mind to stop us connecting with the truth of who we are, which is love. Once we remove those blocks we get to go home. I don't believe it is possible to truly grasp what home is, but deep inside we *know* it. Deep inside we have always felt lonely because of our sense of disconnect. Leading a spiritual life is about being able to connect with a universal picture.

Taking a path of spirit is about making a commitment to loving. If we live on beyond death we have a reason to be good people. There are some people in life that we 'vibe' with; they seem to be on the same level of life path as ourselves. Imagine if you were able to blend energy fully with those people, to be able to merge with them; this is what spirit can do. It's not like losing yourself; it's like becoming part of everything you were already. You might recognize this freeing if you have ever been in love or in fascination with someone. You feel as if you want to consume them, absorb them through your skin. I believe that this is some kind of memory of this blending. Were we once all one being that came apart? My inner knowing feels that to be true, but when I think about it, it seems implausible. Intuition is the key to feeling what the truth of our existence really is – what it is for you. It truly is unknowable because you can only know it as a concept through the workings of the ego, which can only perceive things in terms of 'have' and 'have not.' As you now know, becoming one with everything is a horrific thought to the ego, as it will then have everything and give everything away at the same time.

It really does blow your mind. Have you ever gone too far down the thinking rabbit hole and been told 'best not to think about it,' or 'you think too much.' This is likely to be true. The only thing that can give you an insight into the meaning of life, life after death, or any such matters is to expand your loving consciousness so that you *feel* it. You might never be able to put those feelings into words, but in that moment of connection, it feels tangible. It seems impossible that this energy has an end, like the boundless universe – you change, but you exist beyond the body.

Living an intuitive life has a divine meaning, but it doesn't make you smarter than anyone else or any less likely to experience painful moments in life. To be curious is the only thing that opens the consciousness enough to take the heart with it. Through this gateway we connect intuitively with all that there is, and we find that all that there is, in truth, is love. Living an intuitive life does not get you more sexual partners, next week's Lotto numbers, or international fame; sorry to have not mentioned this sooner in the book, but it does make life easier.

Speed of life

Often people compliment me by saying 'Where do you get all your energy?' 'How do you find the time?' and 'You look like Bridget Jones' (even though I'd rather 'you look like Renée Zellweger' but who cares). Anyway, what's the secret of having time and energy? First, the less time and energy you spend on working out if a decision is right the more quickly you move though life. Also I don't have a TV, TVs suck your time and also give you things to think about that are often irrelevant. I do watch the UK TV show *Doctor Who* and I'm a big sci-fi fan; it opens my mind to time travel and intergalactic possibilities. The clearer your head the more you can hear your intuition (and mute your ego), the easier decisions become, the faster you move the more you get done. My motto is 'Know that you know, know you're right, and move on!' Life is short and living this way feels like living at a divine altitude.

· ·

Intuition for reincarnation

Each lifetime you have lived throughout your existence, you have been given a choice: to choose love or to choose fear. A simple way to explain it is that it is as if you either live your life closed down or full of love, gratitude, and generosity. Fear has many levels and represents itself with many different faces and circumstances. Jealousy, manipulation, cruelty, anger, and vengeance are all aspects of fear. Fear is the underlying cause of everything that doesn't resonate with love. You might not see that it is fear that drives someone to beat someone else up or kill them. The need to destroy an adversary always comes from fear. Bullies at school or in the workplace are scared of the victim and also scared of becoming a victim themselves.

Every fear that you overcome in a lifetime never comes back, as it is part of your ego and no longer has a hold on you. Like peeling the layers of an onion, you move closer to love and remove the blocks to finding the love that has always been within you. Gradually, the real you is revealed. Each lifetime we live, we are only reborn to carry on the task of letting go of the ego (fear). Over and over again we come back and are challenged with a life of metaphors for love and fear. We are faced with things that could trigger us to be the worst of ourselves; we are thrown into testing situations and continually asked, 'Do you choose to respond with love or with fear?'

Choosing love isn't a wishy-washy, limp handshake choice. It is often the hardest choice of all: it's the grown-up, mature choice; it's the choice for the greater good. Sometimes it is the road less traveled, the one where the grass is not worn down by many previous travelers. The road of fear has many passengers going round and round the mountain, while the road of love often shows us that we need to climb the mountain. People call the mountain-climbers crazy. They cannot explain why they need to climb. Life is like being a mountaineer; you feel the passion and the longing for invigoration, which moves you past the fear to being born.

Saying 'yes' to love

Before you were born, I imagine you and I were hanging out in the spirit world. Bobbing around on a cloud, you know the scene! Then the darn nymph with the clipboard came over, looking for the people who had to go back to the physical world to dance again with fear. You jumped up and said 'Me! Me!' Why? You know it sucks to be human; you know the pain of living in ego. As ever, you wanted one more try, so that in one lifetime you could choose love over fear. You react in love not ego. This is enlightenment; when the vibrational frequency that is you is the closest to light, it is also the closest to love. Then and only then can you get back to your real home, a place where all energy is reunited as one. So, one by one we jumped up and said, 'Me! Me! I want a chance to go home.' We knew the pain, but we also knew the exhilaration of that ride was worth it.

Even if we are nailed to a cross, sit under a tree our whole life, or are exiled from Tibet, we keep saying 'yes' to love. Living in a universe that works on polarities, I have often been asked if the worse a lifetime is, the more it takes you closer to your enlightenment. It depends largely on what you choose. You can have the worst things happen to you and make them mean the best things; in other words, you keep finding love in the face of adversity. You can also have the best things happen and they never are enough. I believe each lifetime has a grand purpose or a grand lesson that takes you closer to love. I believe you know it at the time of your death and when you review your life after death. Your enlightenment for this lifetime could be to fall in love, or to be in service to others. Imagine the nymph that came to Princess Diana, when she was just a mere spark of the light of possibility, and said, 'Okay, got a great one for you – you get to live a wonderful and privileged life, but your heart gets broken… a lot. You will die young, leaving two great boys, but you heal the people of a small island called Great Britain and in so doing open its heart chakra, which has been closed since World War II – you know those Brits and their 'stiff upper lip.' This level of sacrifice also means you won't have to be reborn as many times.'

What would you have said to the nymph? What did you agree to do in this lifetime, for your personal growth, the growth of your family, or community? It doesn't have to be bad things; it could be winning gold at the Olympics, writing a life-changing book, bringing a child into the world. We don't know what the large events of our time mean. We don't know if they tip us so far in polarity and take us so close to fear that we then swing harder into love. We don't know the bigger meaning of the disasters and the triumphs of our lives. Even if everything I am saying here is wrong and choosing love makes no difference at all, it still feels better! Freewill is the greatest gift we have ever been given. It is our freewill to continue to destroy the planet and our human existence or to stop and try a different approach. This is the tipping point in our evolution. As individuals, from one lifetime to the next, we get to choose love or fear.

Right now, at this tipping point, our choices as individuals have got to tip the choices of the whole of humanity. It is going to take all of us to think in the same way to change where we are heading. It's not just one of us – it's all of us. Yet each country has a different need from the planet. It is those countries that are in an abundant and privileged position that are going to have to choose love first. Love is the only salvation to the world's problems. All of our lifetimes have taken us up to this point. Of course, many of us are at different stages of enlightenment. And of course, enlightenment isn't a thought, it's a vibration; it's a knowing without words. It is not something you can go out and get, or even look within and find; it's a wordless realization that you are at one with love and always have been.

You know why you're here

You might not have a conscious recollection as to why you are here right now, who you were in your past lives, and what level of enlightenment you are currently working toward. And, even if you don't buy into the idea of reincarnation and the nymph with her infernal clipboard, you'll probably still want to know why you're here – what's your bigger purpose. But your inner knowing knows. The thing is, it knows without words. It might know in images, feeling, or bits and pieces of ideas. The reason for this is so that the ego mind doesn't get hold of the information and use it against you. You can access this knowing in an unconscious way. You might like to do that through imagery, like a form of dreaming. The best way to do it is simply to pose the question. Many people wonder about these things, but never feel it is possible simply to ask. All the answers are inside of you and they have a wonderful way of coming out through the multiple ways of intuitive knowing. Start with becoming curious, which means you're not creating a question that will engage your left hemisphere, but sending out the emotion of curiosity about your past lives or your greater purpose. Try it and see what downloads.

Through the collective consciousness we are all connected. It is therefore possible to connect with the residual energy of your old past life selves. People sometimes feel that this is a place they have never been before. Much of this is unimportant as facts; what is important is that it can give you a sense of connection to everything. You don't see yourself as being part of a time, but timeless. You don't see yourself as being fixed to the roots of your culture, but connected to all cultures and yet knowing your current vibration. You see yourself moving forward into the unknown future with a sense of wonder not fear. You become an all-inclusive energy that embodies the whole world with a consciousness that is tapped into the expanse of the universe. Then you wonder what you want for dinner and you're back in your kitchen.

Being connected won't stop you being an individual while you have an ego at play. It will, however, give you moments when you feel that sense of divinity and bliss, and then you can come back to being you.

Being a historical metaphor

It is my belief, although I have never heard this anywhere else, that there are certain historical figures whose entire lives are a metaphor for human learning. It is a 'knowing' I've had for some time. There was a deeper meaning when Jesus said, 'I died for your sins.' It doesn't fit into my understanding of God because I don't recognize a judgmental God. Yet, when I think of the life of Jesus as a metaphor for us to learn from, it makes sense to me. I believe there are other public figures who seem to have had such extraordinary lives, and it seems odd that only one person would benefit from those experiences. I don't feel time is linear so, in some circumstances, we get to see into someone else's lifetime. If you think about some of the iconic individuals, what would it be like to be able to understand the reasoning behind their decisions? Wouldn't it bring you closer to understanding yourself?

This idea was explored in the movie *Being John Malkovich* when an office worker finds a portal into the subconscious of the actor John Malkovich and witnesses life though his eyes. Imagine being able to step into the shoes of Hitler, Elvis,

Eva Perón, Pol Pot, Gandhi, Mother Theresa or anyone whose life has been extraordinary, whether that life was for the betterment of humanity or not.

Being a witness through an iconic life doesn't mean that we can change history, but it does give us a better understanding of humanity. If you had had this experience in a lifetime, you might feel a resonance with someone from history – maybe a famous actor or political figure. It doesn't mean that you *were* them, just that you might have been almost a walk-in for their life experience. It might have been a whole lifetime or just at a critical moment in time.

States of consciousness

Consciousness is our inner landscape and has many levels: subconscious, conscious, collective consciousness, and super (God) consciousness are some that we have identified and named. Consciousness is part of what it is to be human – to have an internal and natural drive to reach altered states of consciousness. This is because, through the expansion of consciousness, we get to understand the world and ourselves more profoundly. The pull to experience altered states of consciousness is the same as a plant moving toward the sunlight. We are naturally drawn toward what will heal and expand us.

We are also pulled at particular ages in our lives to expand our consciousness: to understand all aspects of who we are, light and shadow. The drive for altered states of consciousness comes when we are teenagers. This is partly why teenagers are so prone to becoming involved in drug and alcohol abuse. I'm not saying that those things heal, but a teenager starts to look for definition of the self.

The drive can also come at midlife when an ordinary person who has lived an ordinary life suddenly needs to experience their shadow self and has what we call a 'midlife crisis,' which might also be called a midlife awakening. A person in midlife might feel the desire for deepened sexual or emotional experiences. They might also seek out meditation or other ways to shift their awareness.

In everyday life we enter in and out of altered states of consciousness. We sleep, stare out of a window in a trance-like state, dance, and lose ourselves in music. Then there is also making love, being in nature, getting angry in a car, etc. – there are so many ways in which we 'lose ourselves.' Being in a state of altered consciousness can feel wonderful, but it can also bring up aspects of ourselves that we don't like to see. This is the shadow (ego) side of human nature. Many seekers of enlightenment don't want to look at the shadow and often want to reach the spiritual, blissful euphoria of enlightenment by bypassing the emotions. Sadly, that isn't sustainable and at some point the shadow will bring you down from your spiritual high as you verbally snap the head off another person for moving your meditation cushion! The shadow coming up is always good news; it just never feels like it, so we shun it. Being in an altered state of consciousness, through meditation, dance, or even certain drugs, amplifies the inner healing, when mixed with authentic living and critical self-inquiry.

Finding meaning

It is what you do with your life in between the spiritual experiences that is really what gives the spiritual experiences the most meaning. All humans naturally gravitate toward wholeness; how they try and find it is an individual experience, but even those who try and find it through wealth will still be taken to a crisis point. We all must face the 'disowned' parts of ourselves, the parts of being human that we deny in ourselves, and judge other people for showing. Facing the disowned parts of ourselves is what it takes to become one and whole. Being naturally pulled toward what will heal us might mean we are pulled toward bad or difficult situations because we will come through the situation with more 'knowing,' which in turn will heal our situation on a deeper perhaps unconscious level. For example, I find that when I go traveling alone, I meet more people. Those people often have something to offer me that I don't have for myself. If I travel with a friend, I don't meet as many people. Whatever we personally need to feed our growth always shows up.

In many traditions, consciousness is understood to be the guiding force in that culture. For example many cultures have a rite of passage for teenagers, to allow them to adjust from the consciousness of child to adult. This creates a safe container in the community for the teenager to go through the transformation they are being pulled toward experiencing.

- On a subconscious level, we always know what we need.

- On a conscious level, we seek to attain it.

- On a collective consciousness level, we know how it affects the whole.

- On a super consciousness level, we know the only thing we are ever really seeking is love.

The consciousness of healing

Believing you need to heal is to believe that there is something wrong with you. There is nothing wrong with you or the world. It would all work perfectly well if we left it alone. But, of course, the structure of humanity would fall apart. Going full circle can bring our needs back to the basic ones. It is the basic, emotional needs of humanity that are not being met: love, peace, and companionship. Yet also, for 80 percent of the world, physical needs are not being met either: food, clean water, shelter, and basic human rights. How can greed have let us get to the point where we allow a person (or millions) to starve right under our noses? The ego can justify anything, even the dire suffering of mankind or the planet. The ego is the insanity of the world's situation, but the more you focus on it, the bigger it becomes. There is something deeper in all of us that is always trying to emerge.

The steps it will take to heal the world are the same steps it would take to heal your life. If people loved you and supported you unconditionally, could you be happy? If everyone had each other's best interests at heart for the bigger picture, would we need capitalism? The ego tips our hand to put ourselves first and our excuse is that we have no other choice, as this is the way the world works. But the world isn't working well. We really want to live in co-existence with the planet. We either choose this or die out – there is really no choice at all. How long it takes us to 'get it' and make the move toward love is as simple as the choices you make every day: whether it is what you buy, what you accept, how you act toward others, or what you think. The steps for global healing are the same as the steps to heal your own life:

- Unconditional love

- Community

- Sharing

- Mindfulness of ego

- Commitment to action for change.

Those are the only things that really matter. Intuition is how we feel safe and know that our unconditional love will not be used against us. Actually it's impossible anyway, but we fear being hurt. Sharing with an open heart comes from knowing when it is right to give and to receive, with the intuition to know when you are coming from your center of balance.

Awakening

When you have these moments of awakening you feel that normality is a waking sleep and these moments feel more real than what we know as reality. I have had these awakened moments throughout my life. This wasn't the first one, but it's one I remember the most. An awakened moment is simply a heightened state of consciousness. People use all kinds of methods to get to a place of expanded awareness and I am no exception: travel, sex, drugs, live music, lighting, dancing, daydreaming, meditation, sailing, walking, singing, dangerous sports, gazing endlessly at hot air balloons. All of these things work to some extent, but the sleep state of normality causes our eyes to dim and we lose our awakened state.

Small moments of awakening

Many years ago I was working as a stage manager on a small show at Edinburgh Festival. I was driving the show's transit van down Princess Street, when something remarkable happened. A bunch of kids were standing on a corner about to throw an egg at the van. The tall one with the egg caught my eye and I impulsively smiled and he smiled back. The whole scene must have taken a moment, but it seemed to last forever. I was in a state of total completeness. Everything seemed full and alive. The repercussions of the feeling lasted a few days, I felt utterly complete. Oh, and he never did throw that egg!

. . . .

There are three stages of awakening. The first is what I experienced in Edinburgh, simply being engaged with the environment. Time seems to stop; you feel part of a flowing motion of life, simple and perfect happiness. The second is when the world becomes really sharp, colorful and vibrant. You are in the moment with a feeling of 'being in love' with everything. You feel as if you are at one with the world and everyone in it. Your mind stops thinking words and you feel a flow of loving energy coursing through your body. The final stage is when you lose track of yourself, you are at one with everything, but there is no 'you.' You have a sense of divine love within, connecting you to everything. You are universal energy and the universal energy is you. You have lost all sense of ego separation; you no longer exist as a separate entity.

Some people believe that these states of awakening are nothing more than the mind playing tricks. Yet when you are in one of these experiences they feel more real than what we commonly call reality. They feel so good that just knowing it is possible to feel like this makes life a remarkable experience.

It seems that the most intense awakenings happen in nature and it is easy to understand why. The natural world causes us to slow down and start observing, whereas it is impossible to take great notice of where you are simply from the volume of fast-moving bodies that surround us in the city. I believe that you have to be out in the trees, the mountains, and by water, to reconnect with yourself, life, and the universal energy. You just need to be able to really see the sky; the expanse of that, itself, can cause an awakening experience. By intuitively tuning in to nature you can create an awakening experience.

But wherever you are, all awakening experiences share one thing in common: you are experiencing the world through your intuitive senses with a lesser connection through ego. You might see intuition as the key to these awakening experiences, or that the awakening itself is your intuition functioning fully. The problem is you can only analyze the experience with hindsight because when you are in the awakening moment, you're not connected enough to your ego to think about it.

When we become numb to life, intuition can wake us back up again. Awakening isn't just about some spiritual enlightenment or a shift of consciousness, it's about choosing life and being alive in that choice.

Life-and-death decisions

You can't know about God, but you can 'know' God. It's hard to come up with a better word than God, but it is linked with so many different ideas defining 'God.' I would like to use the term 'the Knowing' but it sounds like the title of a movie. So let's just stick with God, with the understanding that it is the word used for the energy force of creation. Part of the problem with trying to find the right word for God is that there shouldn't be a word. Words limit and contextualize something that you simply can't understand with the mind. We can know God, but not in a way that can be discussed – only in a way that can be felt. To me, to know God is a form of intuitive knowing, almost like bringing yourself into a place of total stillness from which you are in connection with everything. In that place we no longer have the thoughts of 'this is this and I am that.' It is quite beautiful. Using inner knowing to find God is how we all connect fully.

For many people this connection happens when they are at their lowest ebb, when they are sending out a prayer for God's help, and finally stop the noise in their head to listen for an answer. When the soul-searching moves inward it is because everything external hasn't worked, when there really is nowhere else to turn but inward. Some people have found this moment when a loved one is missing or near death, when they feel that everything in life is lost, when the bills can't be paid, or when they get sick.

Hearing God

The first time I heard God as a form of inner knowing, my mind turned the knowing into words. I was living in Bristol in the UK and involved with a serious drug addict. These scenes often involve a bathroom floor, and this story is no exception. Although God didn't talk to me there, it was here that I decided I was done with life. I was crying and wanting to die. I really wanted to die, as if I could pull my insides out by wishing hard enough.

The next day I moved to London to go to drama school and escape that life but, as I was unpacking my things, I plugged in a desk lamp and experienced a direct current shock – which means you can't let go of the object that is electrocuting you. My arms looked like Mr. Tickle as they went out in front of me. I realized someone would have to shut off the electricity; I looked at a girl standing in front of me and wondered why she wasn't doing anything. I looked into her eyes and saw they were rolled back into her sockets. Then I realized it was me. In that moment I felt a knowing: if I wanted to go home, I could. It was a peaceful idea in a moment of madness. My body however replied 'no' and I made a very odd noise.

My roommate doesn't know why he walked into the room or even if he heard the sound, but within seconds he had disconnected the plug. He himself should have received an electric shock, but somehow that wasn't what happened. My life was saved and I guess, from that moment, I knew that there was something inside and outside of me. Everything that happened came from me; I believe my decision to die caused the circumstances of a possible death, but who provided the calm and safe feeling of death being home?

In the days that followed I was presented with many demons to battle. In my dreams, as well as waking hours, the choice was always the same. It wasn't just a choice in that moment to choose life. It was more than a choice of life or death; it was a choice to live with the full understanding of what life is about. It was a fight of love over fear.

. . . .

Every moment there are only two decisions to make. You can choose love or fear, love or ego. By choosing to live it was a case of fighting fear and to keep choosing love. And if I were to describe my work as an 'intuitive therapist and catalyst' simply, it is to be a guide to make choosing love easier.

TUNING IN TO WHAT YOU KNOW

- Life is about removing the blocks we have created with the ego mind to stop us connecting with the truth of who we are, which is love. Once we remove those blocks we get to go home. We feel lonely because of our sense of disconnect but by choosing to live a spiritual life we are able to connect with a universal picture.

- By living, we keep saying yes to love, every time we are reborn. Every time we step out and do something we are frightened to do, every time we choose to give instead of take, every time we choose to forgive, every time we reach out, or even let go. Love can be found in every decision we make, but especially the difficult ones.

- Love isn't the first choice; self-projection (self-interest) is always the first choice. When you love yourself as a form of love, you are able to move love through you, move wisdom through you, and move inner knowing through you. You become a conduit for everything that you are seeking from somebody else. No one then needs to live up to your expectations of them or to be a benchmark for how you wish to be treated by the world. You flow and bliss flows through you.

Chapter 8
THE INTUITION REVOLUTION

Self-development isn't sustainable without community, and global change isn't possible without community. We need people, but we fear them. Yet we only fear half of them and half of ourselves – we fear the half that protects the physical body, which, as we have discussed, is the ego-governing mind. Love-based intuition can enable us to see people for who they really are, allowing us to connect without fear. By connecting, we can come together in community to make the changes we so desperately need. We are the people we have been waiting for.

But wait; surely it can't be that simple? You get it and I get it, so what about the billions of others who can't get it? In fact, those who are able to read this book are living in privilege. It is a privilege even to be able to say, 'we must change,' when a vast number of people are simply trying to survive.

The human crisis

Humanity is at a time of crisis. We are not changing fast enough to solve the environmental challenges we currently face. In recent years we have seen a rise in natural disasters. We still haven't found a way to end conflict and war. Capitalism and a growth mind-set are destroying the natural world and causing chaos in our communities. Consumerism is the addiction that allows us to continue to destroy. I don't want to depress you, but according to Kevin Danaher, Shannon Biggs, and Jason Mark, the authors of *Building The Green Economy*, no matter what we do now global warming will increase:

- An estimated 6.3 million children suffer from asthma, double the rate of 20 years ago.

- Since World War II, the production of synthetic materials has increased 350 times, and billions of pounds' worth of chemicals have been poured into the environment.

- An estimated 64,000 people die prematurely every year due to the soot from power plants.

The Earth itself breathes with the changing of the seasons. The trees are the lungs of the Earth and the more we cut down trees, the more we make breathing hard for the Earth. Soon we'll make breathing hard for ourselves.

The role of the ego

The 'what-about-me?' ego mind sees the world in separate parts instead of as a whole. This is how the logical mind thinks; it breaks down problems into parts and solves situations bit by bit. This doesn't work; it's a bit like trying to save a vase falling off a table. When you bend to catch it you knock over another vase behind you with your backside. The intuitive mind sees the situation as a whole. When we decide through intuition, with less logic, the right answer for salvation becomes apparent. It is something that we always knew, but put up blocks to seeing it or knowing how to activate it. Love is not a solo activity; we must all love as one. Not understanding how to make someone else feel love not only means that we give up on that person, but in turn we give up on love. Love is the greatest tool for transformation. We must never give up on love; it never gives up on us. As Albert Einstein said: 'The problems that face us cannot be solved at the same level of consciousness that created them.'

Now is the time for the shift of conscious awareness from fear to love.

Which is all very well, but how are you going to convince the rest of the population of the planet? We all want to join in community and fix the problems that affect us, but not with those two, I don't like them, I don't want those two in MY community!

Shifting consciousness

The exciting fact is you might not have to convince anyone of anything. You don't even have to have a verbal revolution toward love; you just have to love and let the rest of the people tune in to your vibration of love. When someone walks into a space in a good or a bad mood, everyone feels it and that person can transform the room positively or negatively.

Through my work with intuition, I have seen people become transformed by changing their mind. Their energy and emotions also shift at the same time. It might be changing our mind about what we have made the past mean, or changing our mind about ourselves; a mental shift causes an energy shift. When I talk at conferences, I see the energy in a room hover over the heads of the people. I sense the connection between everyone listening. I intuitively know that they are all linked into a field of energy that exists outside of the body. As I teach, an 'aha' moment will be collective. It won't just be one person in the room that understands a comment at a deep level, it will be a significant number of people and then the ripple of knowledge spreads out across the room. I then see people scribble notes down, but they miss the wave of energy in the room (I now record my talks for MP3 emails later). Intuitively, I can see a collective consciousness. Comedians also know this; if only a handful of people get a joke, they have to wait a short while and soon the whole room gets it. The understanding of the joke has become contagious, when a moment ago only a few people in the room were tuned into the comedian's wavelength.

The collective unconscious

Now, I don't profess to be a scientist on collective consciousness, so I like to think of this book as an anthology of work done by others on this subject. I started my research when I became a student at the California Institute of Integral Studies, and I really didn't have a logical explanation of what I was expecting to find. I started my inquiry by looking at collective consciousness from the Jungian prospective. I was inspired to do so by a conversation with a fellow student. Isn't this how all great journeys into learning unfold – one coincidental unfolding at a time? Jung describes the collective consciousness as the collective unconscious:

'*My thesis then, is as follows: in addition to our immediate consciousness, which is of a thoroughly personal nature and which we believe to be the only empirical psyche (even if we tack on the personal unconscious as an appendix), there exists a second psychic system of a collective, universal, and impersonal nature which is identical in all individuals. This collective unconscious does not develop individually, but is inherited. It consists of pre-existent forms, the archetypes, which can only become conscious secondarily and which give definite form to certain psychic contents.*'

In summary, the collective unconscious is identical in all humans, meaning that we are all unconsciously linked. This connection exists no matter how far the separation. Many people know who is calling before answering the phone. How many times have you said to someone, 'I was just thinking about you?' Perhaps it is somewhat expected when you know a person, and you could put this down to patterns of behavior or coincidence, but there is more.

Good ideas are 'in the air'

The *New Yorker* ran an article in May 2008 titled *In the Air, Who Says Big Ideas are Rare?* The *New Yorker* claimed that 148 major scientific discoveries were actually multiple independent discoveries, meaning each one was discovered by more than one person working at around the same time. For example:

- Sir Isaac Newton and Gottfried Leibniz both discovered calculus.

- Charles Darwin and Alfred Russell Wallace both discovered evolution.

- Three mathematicians 'invented' decimal fractions.

- In the UK Joseph Priestley discovered oxygen in 1774 and Carl Wilhelm Scheele made the same discovery a year earlier in Sweden.

And they continue: 'That is why we have a patent office – to assign priority since good ideas are 'in the air.' Or we might say 'in the collective consciousness.' Moreover, it is not just humans who seem to share a consciousness. Often animals head to higher ground before a natural disaster such as a tsunami or hurricane, but the story that really clinched this idea for me was *The Hundredth Monkey*.

On the Island of Koshima, scientists were feeding monkeys sweet potatoes but some of them were dropped on the sand. The monkeys liked the taste of potatoes, but not the sandy coating. One of the monkeys, a female named Imo, found she could solve the problem by washing the potatoes in the ocean. Other monkeys soon picked up on Imo's actions and started to copy her; the exact number that started washing the potatoes is not known but the hypothetical number given was 99. Then something startling took place. The number of monkeys washing the potatoes reached a kind of tipping point. The added energy of that 100th monkey somehow created an ideological breakthrough. The habit of washing the sweet potatoes had jumped overseas, and colonies of monkeys on other islands and the mainland began washing their sweet potatoes, too.

I wonder if the missing link in bones between monkeys and humans was created by a shift in consciousness that got us to walk upright and change the way we think?

You might have felt the power of collective consciousness at a music concert or festival. A crowd coming together with one intention is powerful, even if that intention is to have a good time. Many life coach seminars or sales events will invite people to fill a large space for free. These experts get the crowd excited and working together, which creates a collective union. The power of the group dynamic means the person feels amazing, and is very likely to pay lots of money to sign up for the future events, CDs, or books.

There have been experiments on the use of collective positive intention through meditation on the reduction of crime. Transcendental meditation experiments known as the *Maharishi Effect* were conducted in many different cities around the world with positive results. In 1987 a group of 200 people practiced transcendental meditation techniques in Washington DC, which are said to have caused an 11 percent reduction in crime rates.

Remote influence

I was curious to find out if a person could influence another person's feelings and thoughts as an individual to an individual. So I tried this experiment on a work colleague while I was away from our joint-working environment. We had stopped communicating and any attempt I made to talk to her face-to-face, by letter or e-mail was stonewalled. As we both had to work together it was a frustrating situation. So I changed my thoughts from how to solve our situation to thinking about the fun we'd had when our friendship was good. I reconnected with the feelings of friendship and love I still had for her, even though I wasn't a fan of her current choices. When I returned to work and saw her for the first time in a few days, she invited me for coffee. We talked as we had when we were close friends. You could say this was due to us having had time apart, however, she prided herself on never forgiving and letting go of a disagreement, so I believe it was my changed vibration that caused a different reaction from her. All it took was a shift of consciousness. In fact, I have found by sending out my happiness into a room, the atmosphere also shifts to being happy. I have tested being able to change the 'vibe' of a place – from crowded subway trains to my housemates – over and over again and, as long as there are not too many people and I'm in a happy mood, it always works.

The law of resonance

Intuition is listening to sound; people describe it as 'tuning in' or 'reading,' but in essence what you are doing is listening to sound with your whole being and not simply your ears. If we are able to tune in to one thing, such as a person or an object, we are also able to tune in to everything that shares the same resonance. Humanity shares a resonance, as we are all part of the same species. In addition, we think and feel in similar ways. We all share what you could describe as collective consciousness. A person's individual consciousness is directly linked and influences the collective consciousness, and vice versa.

We are all connected through consciousness. The feelings of one person connect with the whole. When we come together and unite over one stimulus, energetic shifts can happen. The energy is contagious, but how does it work? In my book *Advanced Psychic Development* I explain it this way:

> *'Since the moment of the "big bang" everything that exists is actually different forms of energy in vibration. This is what modern science tells us. In real terms, our bodies are composed of the same basic building blocks of matter as everything else. These chemicals have existed in their basic forms (most of them) since they were forged long ago in the bellies of stars. If we look closely at one of these chemical particles, we find that 99.9999% of an atom is nothing but empty space. Within this mostly empty space exist smaller "particles"; protons, neutrons and electrons. These particles are pure energy. Little particles or waves of energy in vibration, actually winking in and out of existence millions of times per second at speeds far beyond the ability of the human senses to detect. Only the most complex scientific equipment can register it. At this subtle level, this **quantum** level of existence, everything consists of tiny packets of energy, and empty space; quantum is the Latin word meaning packet, and you can see how the word quantity came from this root.'*

Energy itself, according to Albert Einstein in his formula $E=MC^2$, is mass (M) multiplied by the speed of light (C) squared. So mass, or matter, when multiplied by the speed of light times the speed of light, equals energy. We know that waves of energy in vibration make sound, so we could say that the whole universe is made of sound, and our thoughts, emotions, and consciousness are also sound. Sound has an interesting quality. If you have a guitar on one side of the room and you strum it, a guitar on the other side of the room, though tuned differently, will resonate to the same frequency as the first guitar. The dominant frequency will tune every other frequency around it and make it vibrate to its own resonance. This is known as 'the law of resonance.' Perhaps this is how our human collective consciousness can spread.

Another similar idea is known as 'morphic resonance.' The person most qualified to talk on this subject is Rupert Sheldrake as published on www.sheldrake.org:

> *'The fields organizing the activity of the nervous system are likewise inherited through morphic resonance, conveying a collective, instinctive memory. Each individual both draws upon and contributes to the collective memory of the species. This means that new patterns of behavior can spread more rapidly than would otherwise be possible.'*

The tipping point

We know that everything works on polarities: it might be fear on one end and love on the other, the North and South poles, or masculine and feminine. Somehow we see these two sides as being separate from each other. Yet one really can't exist without the other. While we see this duality we will always fight one half of ourselves, projecting it out onto others, or using it to focus our attention away from the one truth: love. You can't have darkness where there is light and you can't have a lie where there is truth. It's the same as being unhappy; if you're unhappy about being unhappy you will be twice as unhappy. But if you can be happy about unhappiness, well, then you can't be unhappy. We judge everything to be right or wrong, good or bad. When we love all aspects as one, knowing that each cannot exist without the opposite of itself, then we find that we only have one thing – love.

If you love hate, does hate still exist if it creates love through its existence? The struggle between the ego self and our loving self is a little like the religious fight between the devil and God, as if the two were residing inside every human being. God is love, and love wins your soul when you choose love. What happens when love wins your soul is anyone's guess. Some say we wake up from a dream of duality and go back to being all one. Some call it a shift of consciousness that allows peace on Earth.

All I can tell you is we have reached a crisis tipping point. You might think that things getting worse will tip us toward fear. However, an interesting thing happens: human beings choose. When a bad thing happens we often react to it with a stronger sense of love than fear. When bad things don't happen we stay fearful that they might. I'm not saying we should allow situations to get any worse, but what I do believe is that, in the face of everything that happens, if 51 percent of all people on the Earth choose love we will tip consciousness due to the law of resonance. Of course there are those who believe it could also tip the other way, too, but if there is one thing I believe in it is the transformative power of love.

TUNING IN TO WHAT YOU KNOW

- The intuition revolution gives us survival skills for a changing world. These are exciting times.

- We are in changing times; allow your intuitive knowing to be your guide through all that unfolds.

Most of what we have come to believe will not stay the same. We have already seen a change in the value of money, a lack of loyalty from those we trusted with our financial safety and stability. As times change, your intuition can guide you to make decisions in an uncertain world.

- Therefore, intuition for our future can serve many purposes: to allow us to come together without fear; to intuitively see the problems from a holistic perspective and create sustainable solutions; and give us guidance to make lifesaving decisions when we are faced with crises.

- Most important, your intuition will allow you to open your heart to love and lead you into various states of awakening, which one day might become your view of reality.

Conclusion
YOU *DO* KNOW HOW TO CHANGE THE WORLD

I hope that while reading this book you have had some 'light-bulb moments' that have, perhaps, put some missing pieces together in your learning.

My light-bulb moment happened soon after I moved to San Francisco. As intuition has no words, in all honesty, I thought I was being led to the 'love of my life;' a romantic connection who lived in a house overlooking the ocean. In fact, I did find the most profound love; I found the love I have for myself as I am – the whole of me, warts and all. The me that emerges when that irritating voice in my head isn't trying to change me. In fact, I even loved my inner critic; all the parts of me had a purpose; ego and everything. Nothing needed to change except how I was listening to myself. I realized that nothing had to change in other people except my perception of them, and nothing needed to change in my life except for the belief that a change in my outside world would change my inner feelings.

Why didn't I *know* this before? If I had eaten all the self-help books I had ever read, it would have taken a truck to move me and yet still I didn't know until, following my intuition, I moved to San Francisco and then I knew:

- You can't know self-love with your head, you can only *know* without words.

- You do *know* how amazing you are.

- You do *know* you have potential far greater than the life you're living.

- You do *know* that you can have faith in yourself even if your confidence is knocked.

Stop right now, put your hand on your heart, breathe, and become curious about the power you hold. Become curious about the changes you experience. Allow yourself to open and then be curious about that. Keep going and you'll find you keep on expanding until you get to a point where your eyes are running with tears and you're laughing for having never seen this in yourself before. Really, keep going and you feel as if you are one with everything – one in the whole.

My time in San Francisco also delivered the picture from all the dots I had been putting together for years. The dots I joined together are these:

- Making decisions with love-based intuition means you expand your life because you are supported to make brave decisions.

- You can intuitively get to know the real you beyond your ego self.

- You can open your heart when you trust your intuition to 'see' other people and make good decisions with knowing, not based on psychological beliefs from your past.

- Anything you fear can be parsed by your intuition rather than your ego enabling you to make bold, brave decisions based on your values (rather than what society has told you to value and believe).

- You judge less when you use love-based intuition; it is non-judgmental, it makes sense of the judgment.

- You don't take things personally when you tune in to someone else's reasons for their actions and know that it is rarely about you.

- You open your heart wider and give relationships more understanding when you intuitively know where the other person is coming from.

- When we really learn to listen intuitively we bring patience, love, and understanding to all our relationships – family, lovers, associates and complete strangers – even when their vibration is different from ours.

- Even when the ego is coming up with its objections and fear you can still move forward. You're never going to lose your fear, but you don't have to make decisions in fear.

When you listen with intuitive ears you hear a different world. You become awake to it. You then behave differently. People change how they react to you. Don't believe me? Just try walking around with a smile on your face for half a day, then for the rest of the day look annoyed, you'll soon see. When your community becomes inspired by your change, they will change, too. Due to the law of resonance parts of the world will change until a tipping point is reached.

We *do* know how to change the world and the reason we are not doing it is fear and feelings of separation. Intuition kicks fear into perspective, you might still feel fearful but you act anyway because you *know* it's going to be okay. We feel separate because we are too scared to come together. It is a basic human desire to feel love, not just romantic love but all love; it's the fear that stops us.

Changing your inner landscape: fear to love

Yes we could all sit in our bedrooms and think positive thoughts and that would help shift consciousness, but intuition is the key to shifting your inner landscape into the outside world. Understanding by knowing on the inside is how to react on the outside.

The human being has a marvelous capacity to cope with any kind of living condition and to make it work for them. We are happy to stay in a microcosm of what we know. We often don't question how we know what we know. At the root of how we know what we know is often just a TV commercial, a news broadcast, a conversation, or just the way we were brought up to accept that this is the way it has always been.

For example, I grew up in the north of England, once the center of heavy industry and coal mining in the UK. I remember standing at the end of the road where I lived, watching two of the great chimney towers being demolished with explosives. Factories were part of my landscape, and as a child I didn't think anything of it. I even thought the flames that came out of the chimneys were pretty. I didn't see the big clouds of grey smoke as disturbing. You live with what you know, often in blind acceptance.

It takes a great mind to think outside of these parameters. It takes a leap of consciousness to imagine something else. Perhaps this 'something else' doesn't even exist yet. Everything that exists started in someone's imagination, often building on someone else's creation. We know how to build and reshape, but we don't seem to know how to tone down and do less. The closure of the factories and coal pits in the north of England caused massive unemployment and hardship in the 1970s and 80s but, as ever, the region mostly bounced back, became creative and found different avenues. For example, Manchester flourished and became a hub for new music in the 1990s, and many of the slag heaps were landscaped into healthy, vibrant, recreational parks.

It is my belief, from reading all of the information, that until we intuitively relook at what we already know, we can't see the bigger picture of how the world could be reshaped to become sustainable. We fear this kind of change, but we forget who we are because the average human being has an immense capacity to cope with any kind of living condition and make it work.

Over the next few years we are likely to feel as though we are in a bottleneck. We've had plenty of space so far, but in order to fit through the neck of the bottle and find real freedom we're going to have to let go of many of the things we once found to be important. We will likely try to hang on to what we have and push with our shoulders and elbows, trying to keep hold of our fake values. If we do that, we will keep slipping down the bottle and only make things harder for ourselves. The bottleneck is a birth canal and you can't be born without letting go of your stuff. You have to shed layers of your ego until you are small enough to fit through the gap. It might be painful, but only if you fight it. We can't predict the future, but you can choose to imagine and let go of old patterns. The rug cannot be pulled out from under you when you're dancing on it. Bracing and holding on will only see you landing flat on your behind.

Seeing the world with intuitive eyes

We can change; we just need to start looking at things with a fresh set of eyes. These new eyes are intuitive and full of curiosity. When a person goes traveling to a new place, they are curious about it. They meet the most wonderful people and experience the most amazing coincidences. When we are home, we don't look through the same curious eyes; home seems dull. But if we do look around us with curiosity we find coincidences occurring, we meet marvelous new people, we make connections that serve our purpose, and we find new romantic partners.

We are like the traveler who, with one small shift, becomes curious. When we are curious we find messages in the world, and answers to questions before we even ask. Life is like the cloud that passes overhead, its shape reminding us of a bunny rabbit and making us smile. Become curious about why you are seeing a rabbit and you'll find the cloud works like a tarot card. Intuitive information is in everything that the right hemisphere of your brain can access, showing you a message from your higher consciousness. When you use intuitive eyes and ears, you overhear a conversation on the train differently, and see that a ripped-up bag has a meaningful shape. Life becomes exciting, full of wonder, and above all magical.

With this new set of eyes comes a new set of actions. When you change one person's emotions the law of resonance means there is a knock-on effect to the whole of humanity. Simply being kind can be a tipping point. Give to others the same kind of values you would wish for in a perfect world. Use your imagination and ask yourself: 'What in my current reality isn't as important as it should be?' Then imagine a new one and live life as if this version of reality was the correct one.

Whether a decision was brave or stupid can only be decided with hindsight. Choose to be brave as the chances are it will never turn out to be stupid. If you don't like your past, rewrite it; be more positive, because you're no longer living in the past, but your memory of it. As we know, memory can be faulty, so what's wrong with changing the past so that it has a more positive effect on your present beliefs?

Intuition gives you all of the answers you have been running around trying to find. They are already inside you, waiting to emerge. The ego would like to keep you running like a headless chicken, as your emerging love dissolves the ego layer by layer. You were born at this time for something important; you feel it inside. When you hear this you assume it is your ego talking but it is your awareness; it's your ego that tells you it's your ego! You are here to shift perspective toward love and away from fear. This is your purpose. You can do it anywhere, living any life. All you need to do is choose love in any situation. Love doesn't get abused, it just kindly points out its choice to keep you moving toward it and not to be pulled down by others' fear. It's the simplest revolution in the world; it doesn't need red flags, marching bands, or guns. It doesn't need strong conversations or megaphones on street corners. It just needs us to choose love and to keep choosing it.

While the world is in this transition toward love over ego, our intuition works as a bridge. Using intuition we can see behind a person's ego to their loving self. We don't have to talk to the head, we talk to the heart, and we can hear the heart beating behind whatever is said. Our intuitive heart empowers others to come from the heart and not the ego, too. We will live in a mixed-up society for a while, but when you are not mixed up you can become part of the tuning vibration of love. Until we reach the tipping point and live in harmony, think about it: what can you do to make the world a better place?

Laugh a lot and have a really good time. Enjoy life. Love yourself and others and if you're struggling with any of that, become curious and use intuition to find out why. Be happy, that's the best you can be for everyone else.

JOIN THE HAY HOUSE FAMILY

As the leading self-help, mind, body and spirit publisher in the UK, we'd like to welcome you to our family so that you can enjoy all the benefits our website has to offer.

 EXTRACTS from a selection of your favourite author titles

 COMPETITIONS, PRIZES & SPECIAL OFFERS Win extracts, money off, downloads and so much more

 **LISTEN** to a range of radio interviews and our latest audio publications

 CELEBRATE YOUR BIRTHDAY An inspiring gift will be sent your way

 LATEST NEWS Keep up with the latest news from and about our authors

 ATTEND OUR AUTHOR EVENTS Be the first to hear about our author events

 **iPHONE APPS** Download your favourite app for your iPhone

 HAY HOUSE INFORMATION Ask us anything, all enquiries answered

Join us online at **www.hayhouse.co.uk**

 292B Kensal Road, London W10 5BE
T: 020 8962 1230 E: info@hayhouse.co.uk

ABOUT THE AUTHOR

Becky Walsh is an intuitive catalyst for people who want growth and positive change in any area of life. She has a private practice for consultations in Bristol and London, and also over the phone and via Skype. Best known for having had a radio show on LBC 97.3, she is also the author of two published books – *Advanced Psychic Development* and *Intuitive Lovers* – six e-books, and numerous online courses.

Becky teaches all over the world including Pakistan, Hong Kong, the USA, the UK, and Chile. She also is a spiritual performance artist and regularly performs her stand-up intuitive show.

Becky is a director of openbeyond.com, a platform that supports self-development teachers and their students.